Tips for Teaching Kids with Asperger's

Practical Strategies to Help Teachers Improve School Success for Students with Asperger's Syndrome

by
Marjorie Pike
and Kelly Gunzenhauser

illustrated by
Alex Patrick Shimkus

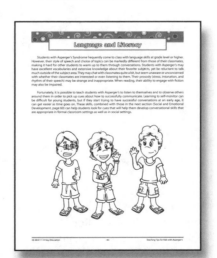

Key Education Publishing
An imprint of Carson-Dellosa Publishing, LLC
Greensboro, North Carolina

keyeducationpublishing.com

CONGRATULATIONS ON YOUR PURCHASE OF A KEY EDUCATION PRODUCT!

The editors at Key Education are former teachers who bring experience, enthusiasm, and quality to each and every product. Thousands of teachers have looked to the staff at Key Education for new and innovative resources to make their work more enjoyable and rewarding. We are committed to developing educational materials that will assist teachers in building a strong and developmentally appropriate curriculum for young children.

PLAN FOR GREAT TEACHING EXPERIENCES WHEN YOU USE EDUCATIONAL MATERIALS FROM KEY EDUCATION PUBLISHING

About the Authors

Marjorie Pike is an elementary school teacher with a master's degree in teaching. She has been a reading specialist and has worked with children on the autism spectrum for 16 years. Marjorie is married and the mother of two boys.

Kelly Gunzenhauser teaches two-year-olds. She has a master's degree in English and has been an editor and writer in the educational publishing field for over 13 years. She is an avid school volunteer. She lives in Winston-Salem, North Carolina, with her husband and two active kids.

Dedications
For my teachers Emery, James, and John.
–M. P.

For my wonderful brother and teacher, David.
–K. G.

Credits
Authors: Marjorie Pike and Kelly Gunzenhauser
Project Director: Sherrill B. Flora
Illustrations: Alex Patrick Shimkus
Editor: Claude Chalk
Layout Design: Key Education Production Staff
Cover Photograph: © Shutterstock

Key Education
An imprint of Carson-Dellosa Publishing, LLC
PO Box 35665
Greensboro, NC 27425 USA
keyeducationpublishing.com

ISBN 1-978-162057-368-6
01-002138091

Introduction

Asperger's syndrome is one of a number of developmental disorders on the autism spectrum. It affects motor skills, sensory abilities, communication abilities, and social skills. Students with Asperger's may have near-normal or even exceptional intelligence and are often able to function well in mainstream classrooms. Therefore, as a preschool or elementary school teacher, it is likely that you will spend a school year with a student who has been diagnosed with Asperger's.

Not every student who exhibits Asperger's-like behaviors has Asperger's. It is certainly possible that you will have students who have some of the behaviors and characteristics of Asperger's, but who do not fully meet the diagnosis criteria. Still, other students may receive diagnoses in the future but for the time being are in your classroom. Without the diagnosis, no additional services are offered to these students.

Some typical Asperger's behaviors and characteristics can be challenging to manage, but Asperger's can bring certain gifts as well. For example, while these students may have difficulty with social awareness or motor skills, they may also have a deep understanding of favorite subjects, possess high intelligence, and strive to find loving relationships. Teaching a student with Asperger's can take extra energy on your part because you may have to modify many of your lessons. You may also need to spend more time on behavior management. But, it can also be highly rewarding and enriching to have such a student in your classroom.

Tips for Teaching Kids with Asperger's is a useful tool that offers simple and efficient strategies to even out the amount of time you spend on a student(s) with Asperger's and the rest of the students in your classroom. This book helps you identify specific challenges with each student with Asperger's (because they are all so different), offers a variety of solutions for each challenge, and even gives advice for partnering with the student to overcome these challenges. Because the book focuses on modifying behaviors and building skills, you are certain to find hints for helping students who exhibit some of these behaviors and characteristics but who do not belong on the autism spectrum—which means less planning for you. Best of all, *Tips for Teaching Kids with Asperger's* also offers ideas for fostering tolerance and empathy in your classroom community.

Table of Contents

PART ONE – Welcome to the Spectrum: Terms and Abbreviations

You will not come across most of these terms frequently in this book, but you will find them if you do any research about Asperger's syndrome and possibly when dealing with parents and counselors.

- **Asperger's Syndrome:** A developmental disorder that affects a person's ability to communicate and socialize with others. Symptoms vary but may include repetitive speech, behavioral rituals, difficulties with recognizing and interpreting nonverbal communication, and some motor difficulties.

- **Aspie:** A term used by some members of the Asperger's community as an abbreviation for Asperger's; also refers to individuals diagnosed with this syndrome.

- **Autism Spectrum:** Traditionally, the Autism Spectrum has encompassed five specific disorders: autism, Asperger's syndrome, pervasive developmental disorder-not otherwise specified (PDD-NOS), Rett's syndrome, and childhood disintegrative disorder. All are related disorders with mostly unknown causes that affect social and communicative skills, cognitive skills, and motor function.

- **Diagnostic and Statistical Manual of Mental Disorders [(DSM IV-TR (2000)]:** This is the guidebook of the American Psychiatric Association that catalogs all mental disorders. At the time of this writing, the American Psychiatric Association is in the process of revising the DSM IV-TR. In the next edition, Asperger's will be grouped together with other disorders under the broader term Autism Spectrum Disorder. We are retaining the term Asperger's in this publication at this time for descriptive purposes.

- **Neurotypical (NT):** This refers to a person who does not have Asperger's or another autism spectrum disorder.

Using This Book

You probably will not read *Tips for Teaching Kids with Asperger's* cover to cover; rather, you will use it as a reference. Inside you will find practical advice and suggestions for documenting, troubleshooting, and problem-solving many of the unique situations that may arise when you teach a student on the autism spectrum in a mainstream classroom. This book contains a collection of ideas and strategies for helping students with Asperger's, as well as their classmates and teachers, to have the best possible experience in your classroom.

Consider a sample scenario: Mike is a student with a diagnosis of Asperger's. You met briefly with his parents before the start of the school year. One thing you learned about him is that he loves airplanes—and will talk about them constantly no matter what the topic of conversation. Something else you learned is that his parents are worried about his reading. He likes to read only nonfiction books about airplane parts. His parents also tell you that Mike only eats crackers with cheese for lunch and that loud noises are stressful for him.

You can flip through this book to read about obsession with one subject (page 47), reluctance to read fiction or read outside of a comfort zone (page 52), having tangential conversations (page 84), rigidity with diets (page 37), and aversion to loud noises (page 34), because all of these apply to Mike. Next, you could search for some fictional stories about airplanes.

During the school year, you notice that Mike is arguing a lot with you and his classmates. You flip to page 103 to find strategies for dealing with the arguing. You make notes on a copy of the Behavior Documentation and Action Record Form on page 11, citing which strategies you try and describing successes and failures. Eventually, you will hit on a strategy that seems to lessen the arguing.

At the end of the year, you can look back on Mike's progress. He is still struggling a little with arguing, and he still only likes to read about airplanes, but he has learned a lot about some other things and has made some good friends. You know that while you may not have done everything right, at least you were armed with some strategies to deal with what you knew was coming (dislike of loud noises, food sensory issues, perseveration about airplanes) and what popped up (arguing excessively). Using this book will help you be prepared for what is coming and can also help you manage any surprises.

Using the Teacher Worksheets

The following teacher worksheets can make your life easier. Read ahead to see how to use them to schedule and analyze your day, explain your day to substitute teachers, and evaluate and manage challenging student behavior.

Daily Schedule (page 8)

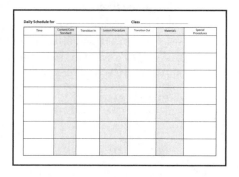

You will likely have official schedules and planning forms provided for you through your school system, but this schedule can be helpful if you have a student with Asperger's syndrome. Transitions can be very difficult for students who have Asperger's. A traumatic transition time can ruin the student's entire day and everyone else's too. (See pages 16–17 for more about transitions.) The Daily Schedule helps you plan routines to make these transitions easier. The schedule can be especially helpful at the beginning of the year or on days when the routine is out of the ordinary, such as when you are demonstrating a science experiment or there is a special event at the school.

Different students will need different kinds of transitions. As you try each one and then discard it because it is not working, keep the pages as a record of the various strategies you have tried. When it is time to come up with new transition strategies for another new student, you can go back to these instead of having to think up new ones.

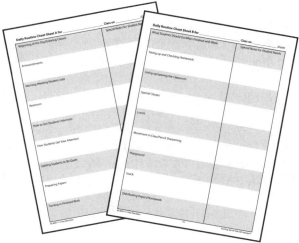

Daily Routine Cheat Sheets (pages 9–10)

Having a substitute teacher in your classroom is an adventure at the best of times, both for the teacher and your students. On the Routine Cheat Sheets, fill in information under the headers to walk a substitute through the day. You can also add notes about special accommodations that will help your substitute work smoothly with your student with Asperger's.

Behavior Documentation and Action Record Form (page 11)

Behavioral incidents always require careful documentation. Anecdotal recollections long after the fact are usually far less accurate than recording specific events on the dates that they happen. When you have specific, concrete information and dates for several incidents, you can spot behavior patterns more easily. Spotting patterns gives you crucial information that can help you reduce the number of events in your classroom. The reason is that there may be specific triggers that are hard to spot without plenty of documentation. Also, you can take concrete information to a professional, such as a school counselor, who may be able to help you analyze the information and come up with solutions.

For example, without dates, you may notice that a student always seems to act out in the morning, but you may not realize that it is always on Tuesday morning just before music class. This is significant information. Using the Behavior Documentation and Action Record Form, you can record the exact date and time, and the exact behaviors, to see if it is related to music class or to something that happens beforehand. You can also record each action you take to try to reduce the behavior, as well as the results, on the Behavior Documentation and Action Record Form, and analyze what is working and what is not. Using specific, concrete information about the times and days of the behavior, what the student does, and what you do, will be much more helpful in developing effective strategies.

Daily Schedule for _____

Class _____

Time	Content/Core Standard	Transition In	Lesson Procedure	Transition Out	Materials	Special Procedures

Tips for Teaching Kids with Asperger's

KE-804111 © Carson-Dellosa

-8-

Beginning of the Day/Entering Classes	Special Notes for Student Needs
Announcements	
Morning Meeting/Student Jobs	
Restroom	
How to Get Students' Attention	
How Students Get Your Attention	
Getting Students to Be Quiet	
Preparing Papers	
Turning in Finished Work	

Daily Routine Cheat Sheet B for _____ **Class on** _____ *(Date)*

What Students Should Do When Finished with Work	Special Notes for Student Needs
Taking Up and Checking Homework	
Lining Up/Leaving the Classroom	
Special Classes	
Lunch	
Movement in Class/Pencil Sharpening	
Playground	
Snack	
Distributing Papers/Homework	

Behavior Documentation and Action Record Form for _____

Date/Time	What Was Happening at the Time	Student's Behavior	Action Taken	Analysis/Results

KE-804111 © Carson-Dellosa

Tips for Teaching Kids with Asperger's

Teachers love to cover their walls with job charts, student art, behavior modification posters, popcorn words, and other resources. Preschool teachers cover walls of their pre-reading classrooms with environmental print, shapes, colors, weather charts, calendars, and pictures. A busy environment and constant change can overwhelm students with Asperger's. However, it is well known that most students' brains are stimulated by change and variety, and that many do find posted resource materials helpful. Stripping the room completely is not the best option. Think carefully about configuring and decorating your classroom and use the information below to find a balance and meet all students' needs.

Room Furniture

Preschool and kindergarten classrooms usually have tables. They are more manageable than desks, and it is easier to control access to supplies rather than have students try to keep up with them in desks. Older students' classrooms often require desks. They can be more disruptive because they slide more easily, and supplies can get disorganized. But, there is more flexibility with classroom arrangements. When arranging furniture, consider the following ideas.

- **Think about spacing between students.** Students with Asperger's may talk to themselves or touch other students, or be especially protective of their things. Consider moving the student with Asperger's a bit away from others to relieve stress and limit distractions.

- **Try not to seat the student by the door.** Visitors are a distraction, and you also want to make sure the student is not tempted to impulsively leave the room if the door is open. (This is not a problem for all students with Asperger's.)

- **Background noise.** Find out from parents (or from your observations) whether the student is bothered by background noises that most people do not notice, such as buzzing fluorescent lights or electronics. Seat the student away from the computer center if possible. If you cannot isolate the student from a bothersome noise, earplugs or headphones may help.

- **Light sensitivity.** Students with Asperger's may be light sensitive or may be easily distracted by outside activity. Seat the student away from the direct light and the distracting pull of windows.

- **One-piece, desk-and-chair model.** If the student has trouble managing a separate desk and chair, substitute an old-fashioned, one-piece, desk-and-chair model. Joined pieces of furniture are more stable than two separate pieces.

- **Quiet areas.** From time to time, any student may need a quiet place to recharge or settle down. A student with Asperger's is highly likely to need such a place. Designate a quiet area in the room away from other seating areas. Stock it with pillows, books, an exercise ball to sit on, and other comforting objects.

Classroom Walls

Classroom walls offer encouragement, humor, and a wealth of information and reference for students. They also reflect your personality. However, busy walls can overwhelm students with Asperger's. As you choose what to put on your walls, keep the idea of balance in mind.

- **Unclutter.** As you prepare your classroom for the year, start by uncluttering the walls and surfaces (tabletops and cabinet tops). Add back necessary items only. Make sure you give the eyes a place to rest by leaving plenty of white space and clean surfaces.

- **Make wall decorations count.** Hang things students actually need, such as charts of sight words, colors and shapes, alphabet letters, hundreds boards, attendance board, job chart, and maps.

- **Students with Asperger's may become attached to or fixated on things they see every day,** including wall decorations. If you find that a student is very attached to a poster or picture on the wall, try to leave it there.

- **If possible, complete your room decorating before Open House** so that there are no surprises on the first day of school.

- **Hang art in the hallway if possible.** You can also designate cabinet doors or a dark bulletin board as student art space so that there is not so much contrast against a white wall.

- **Always display artwork in the same place.** It won't seem like such a big difference when it changes.

- **Let students participate.** Let them choose what to display or help you arrange the artwork you pick out so that they have some control over the changes in that space.

Materials and Storage

Organization can be a special challenge for students with Asperger's, and indeed for many young students. Teaching organization is a gift you give to students that they will use all of their lives. Use these ideas to keep students from getting overwhelmed with their own things.

- **Tables can be best.** Tables help eliminate having students with Asperger's trying to organize their own materials. Desks are more problematic because students must manage their own materials. If you have desks, be prepared to develop systems to help the student with Asperger's stay organized.

- **Keep a small storage box at your desk.** Using a pencil pouch or box can be difficult for some students. Materials can get lost or broken, or are so numerous that they are overwhelming. Sometimes, it is better to keep a small storage box at your desk and let the student retrieve the one thing he needs and then replace it.

- **Sending papers between home and school.** Paper clutter can be a challenge for all students, not just those with Asperger's. You probably already have a system in place for sending home papers and taking them back in. Review your system carefully with this student and his parents and occasionally check behind him to make sure papers are not piling up.

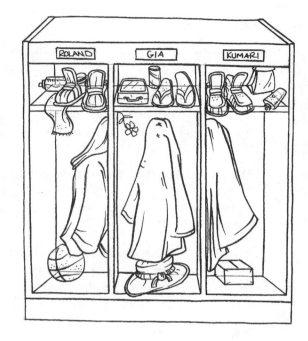

- **Organize personal belongings.** Other personal belongings often fare better when they are kept in a central location instead of at students' desks. Most students cannot manage large jackets, and they may be tempted to take out their lunches before lunchtime. Designate classroom space for lunch boxes, coats, and other items from home. Consider using wall hooks, open shelves, or stacked file organizers or shoe cubbies to help students keep their belongings organized.

- **Store things not frequently used.** Seeing stacks of games, puzzles, toys, overflowing books, and boxes of manipulatives can really distract students. Classrooms need more storage to appear less cluttered. You may need to rotate more items out of the classroom in order to keep items out of sight. Students should only be able to see what they use regularly, so plan to store things students are not using.

- **Cover open bins and shelves.** If you must store overflow items in the classroom, cover open bins and shelves with tablecloths or curtains. Use solid fabrics in muted colors—busy patterns are distracting too.

- **Enlist students' help in keeping the classroom in order.** They need to be responsible for putting away books and games, straightening their personal belongings and supplies, and cleaning up the floor at the end of the day.

- **For more information about keeping materials and projects organized,** see the Disorganization section on page 115.

When You Have to Make a Change

Despite change being difficult, you will certainly want to move students' seating or artwork around during the year as your needs and students' needs change. These ideas will help make room changes less disruptive for students.

- **Post the daily schedule** and the morning message each day, using a pocket chart and pictures, if you can. Review the schedule each morning and note any changes that will happen that day.

- **Consistent seating placement.** When possible, change other students' seats, but leave the student with Asperger's in the same seat as long as it is working for him.

- **If you change seating in the classroom,** think about what is the best course of action. You may warn students ahead of time, but this may cause anxiety until the change happens. It may be best to change seats after school one day and then give a "tour" of the changes the next day, pointing out the positives as you go.

- **Scheduling any changes** you plan to make to the classroom ahead of time can be one way to make them less stressful. For example, you may plan to change artwork or a bulletin board or the seating arrangement on the first Monday of every month. If you post this on your calendar, explain it to the students and remind them about it. It will feel less like a change and more like part of the routine.

- **Consider asking the student who fears change to help you make the changes.** Have the student arrange new student artwork, pick out the new border for a bulletin board, or draw a bird's-eye view of the new desk arrangement. Some students have excellent color vision or spatial awareness and can be quite helpful with their drawings. Plus, making a bird's-eye-view drawing may give them some feeling of being "on top of" the changes.

- **Learning to cope with change.** Finally, even though change can be stressful for a student with Asperger's, that student also has to get used to not being able to control everything. Part of learning to successfully cope with Asperger's is learning to cope with change, so bear in mind that you are helping the student learn life skills by dealing with new words on the popcorn word chart or having a different seatmate.

Now, with your classroom ready, you can finally greet your students. If you do have a student with Asperger's joining your classroom, what can you expect from this student? The fact is, even if you have had a meeting with parents and know some of the student's potential behaviors ahead of time, there is no way to know exactly what to expect. The student may act very differently in a classroom setting, just as all other students behave differently at home than they do at school. And, all students with Asperger's are different from each other as well. However, they do tend toward a broad collection of possible behaviors, skills, and challenges, and that is what the rest of this book deals with.

For the remainder of this book, you will find a list of behaviors and characteristics under the following categories: Physical Development, Language and Literacy Development, Social and Emotional Development, and Personal Responsibility. These behaviors encompass many of the things you might see when teaching your student with Asperger's, and also the reactions of classmates. While in many cases you may not be able to stop the behavior, you may be able to lessen or improve it, or at least increase your own understanding of and patience with it, as well as fellow students' empathy toward it. The more you can make this student's behavior seem ordinary to classmates, the easier things will be for everyone in your classroom.

Special Considerations as You Start the School Year

Teaching a student with Asperger's in your classroom is both challenging and rewarding and requires thought and planning. Here are two more things to consider when you know you have a student with Asperger's entering your classroom.

1. Using the Word "Asperger's"—or Not

All teachers are taught to be especially sensitive to families who have children with disabilities, especially when you think there is a disability and a family does not. If the family does not come to you with a label, then it is not appropriate to use one. This is certainly true with students with Asperger's. Students with Asperger's can go to either extreme, so it is best to know the situation. Some students are diagnosed early and embrace the term and diagnosis. A student may be proud to be an "Aspie." Other students have no understanding of their diagnosis. Or, they or their families may be aware that some of their behavior is "spectrum-like" but have no wish to associate themselves with a label. Make sure you get to know your individual student and the family before you start using the terminology with them, and of course, do not use a label in front of classmates. If the student decides to label himself as an Aspie in class, discuss this with the family and find out your school's policy before you decide how to address it.

2. Transitions Are Tricky

Transitions will come up a lot in this book because they are the times when many other behaviors occur. Many students—even neurotypical ones—have a hard time with transitions. With transitions come uncertainty, and uncertainly is difficult. Often, transitioning is harder at the beginning of the year, but once a student knows that P.E. is always on Monday, Art is always on Tuesday, and lunch is always at 11:15, then transitions become less stressful. But, what if the art teacher gets sick? What if the children's symphony gives a special concert? And, what if a substitute has to take over your room for the day? Because a student with Asperger's is also likely to be pulled out of the classroom for special services, you have a recipe for constant change.

Students who fear transitions may be reluctant to change activities during class or resist leaving the classroom. They may frequently ask what is coming next. To soothe themselves, they may flap hands or talk to themselves any time they think change is coming. Or, they may obsess over change, even if they know the outcome. For example, a student may refuse to go outside for a late recess because he is afraid of not hearing his bus number called, even though his teacher constantly reassures him that she will let him know when it is time to come in. These behaviors may subside during the school year, but they may remain; the student may have very little control over them. You must be patient and flexible and realize that the behaviors are not born out of stubbornness or defiance, but out of a high level of anxiety, and that the student is trying to control the situation with actions like refusing to go to the playground.

Solutions to Help the Student Reduce His Anxiety and Adapt Better to Transitions

- **Each day, review the schedule briefly and then explain when there will be exceptions to the rule** such as different classes or visitors. You can promise to let the student know what is coming as often as possible, and he can promise to trust you and let you know when he is upset.

- **Work out a signal that the student can use to show you that she is anxious about an upcoming transition,** such as waving at you, leaving a note on your desk, or turning over a card. (Allow the student to keep a card on his desk that is green on one side and red on the other. He can turn the red side faceup when he needs help.) You can give him extra reassurance quietly at his desk without embarrassing him in front of the class.

- **Schedule out-of-class therapies.** When a student with Asperger's gets pulled out of class for different therapies, it can throw him off. Consider talking with resource teachers or your school administration about carefully scheduling therapy time out of class if you think that it is especially disruptive for this student. Also, consider altering your in-class schedule. For example, schedule free reading time when the student is out of class so that he does not miss any favorite activities or direct instruction, and ask the student's parents to have extra free reading time at home.

- **Build in signals so that everyone knows a transition is coming.** Turn off lights, ring a bell, sing a song, play some music, or use another gentle signal so that students can start the transition on their own by packing away their things. Consider letting students take turns signaling the transition, starting with the student with Asperger's, if it will make him feel he has more control over the transition.

- **Make transitions fun.** Pretend you are going somewhere interesting when you walk down the hall. Shake your sillies out before doing a new subject if your transition is only happening in class. Take five minutes to do the "Hokey Pokey." Do whatever works.

- **For students who have favorite and least favorite subjects,** try to schedule the least favorite first and transition to the favorites. Most students will be eager to move on to something they like.

Physical Development

Students with Asperger's syndrome often exhibit delayed or awkward physical development. Their gross motor skills may make sports and large muscle activities difficult for them, which can undermine their confidence and ability to fit in at school. A lack of fine motor skills can affect handwriting and other academic tasks.

Beyond those issues, motor skill limitations can extend to things such as spatial awareness and directionality, which affect how easily a student moves and finds her way around. She may also use repetitive motions such as rocking to comfort herself, have tics, or have sensory issues that make certain physical experiences difficult for her.

Because a student with Asperger's cannot always master motor skills with ease, and cannot always control her reactions to sensory input, it is important to understand how each student's particular physical makeup will affect her academic and social experiences at school. Use the ideas in this chapter to help you identify and troubleshoot some of the physical difficulties that can accompany Asperger's.

Poor Fine Motor Skills

Poor fine motor skills will cause students to have poor handwriting and have trouble completing schoolwork. Nothing ruins a good assignment like not being able to read what a student has written or having a student cut off his answer on a cutout page. Watch for these signs that a student is struggling with fine motor skills.

Indicators of Poor Fine Motor Skills

- After age four, shows no strong hand dominance (does not seem to prefer to use his right or left hand).

- Has difficulty properly gripping a pencil or crayon.

- Has poor hand strength.

- Avoids fine motor tasks or cannot sufficiently perform activities such as zipping clothing, cutting, building block towers, etc.

- Cognitive performance suffers because of poor fine motor skills. (For example, cannot demonstrate math skills on worksheets because of poor performance on color-by-number and cut-and-paste worksheets.)

- Dislikes computer activities or seeks a partner to work the mouse.

- Handwriting finesse lags far behind that of classmates.

Tips and Tricks for Improving Fine Motor Skills

- **For students who enjoy the playground, blacktop, or gym, provide fine motor tools to entice them into participating.** Sidewalk chalk, bubbles, jump ropes to untangle and turn, and textured balls will help increase hand strength and dexterity.

- **Modify some of your pencils for students who have trouble gripping.** Purchase "fat" pencils or pencil grippers, or let students squeeze modeling clay around their pencils.

- **Let students use tiny pencils** such as golf pencils for a fun change. Gripping a smaller pencil will strengthen hand muscles and encourage proper pencil grip.

- **Read, write, and walk.** In elementary school, have students "read" the classroom using small notepads and pencils. As they walk around, they should write down words they see. This adds a motion element to writing. If you pair students with partners, it adds a social aspect as well.

- **Provide many choices for writing utensils** and encourage your young writers to use them in their regular writing. Sometimes, all students need to tackle a writing assignment is permission to decorate it with stickers, choose colored paper, highlight words with markers, and draw with colored pencils or pens.

- **Have a parent send in cheese cubes and small pieces of fruit for snacks.** Before beginning any food activity, ask families' permission and inquire about students' food allergies and religious or other food restrictions.

- **Using clothespins or tweezers,** have students pick up small, soft objects such as cotton balls.

- **Let students use eyedroppers and spray bottles** for painting projects to strengthen their pincer grips and hand muscles.

- **Have a note-writing day in your classroom.** Let students write (or pretend to write) notes to each other and pass them in class. Share some of your best note-folding techniques.

- **If possible, set up a gift-wrapping or post office station in your classroom.** Folding paper, dispensing tape, and stuffing envelopes are great fine motor activities.

- **Folding paper can be frustrating** to students with Asperger's. When edges do not line up perfectly, the lack of perfection can be highly frustrating. Make sure that folding activities are simple and include step-by-step instructions with pictures. Always be prepared to help. Triangle-shaped paper footballs are a great first-time paper-folding project.

- **Make Your Own Paper Airplane worksheet (page 22).** Make paper folding rewarding by using the Make Your Own Paper Airplane worksheet for practice. Let students practice folding by creating flying machines in the classroom. Then, have a designated flying day inside or outside the classroom. (Pre-readers and younger students will need help with the directions. To avoid frustration, you may want to demonstrate this activity first and then have parent volunteers available to help as students fold their own.)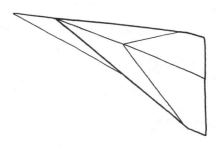

- **Computer mice.** Let students work with partners until they are more comfortable using the computers in your classroom or computer room. For extra practice, ask parents or a local thrift ship to donate old keyboards and mice for students to play with.

- **Think outside of the box for art projects.** Explore torn-paper and found-object collages, weave fabric strips, squeeze out glitter glue, make art with stamps or stencils, create sticker pages, punch holes and use the confetti for art, or punch holes in cardboard and do lacing activities.

- **Fine motor manipulatives.** Purchase peg boards with lacing strings, bead jewelry sets, linking cubes, and other small construction and drawing sets. Students will find them more "grownup" and appealing than the counters used for sorting and fine motor practice in preschool.

- **Create collage art projects** with small objects and glue. Beans, torn paper, buttons, sprinkled sand, gravel, and other tiny objects will challenge little fingers.

- **Magic Learning Center.** Students in first grade and up are ready for a little magic. A simple magician's kit with instructions will fascinate some students, and the sleight-of-hand tricks are great for improving fine motor skills. This can make a great free-time center in your classroom.

- **Using play dough and clay** with small cookie cutters builds strength in fingers, but be aware that the smell of play dough may bother some students with Asperger's.

- **For those who love construction,** provide nuts and bolts for them to take apart and put back together.

- **Sensory table.** Some students with Asperger's may crave textural stimulation, while others cannot tolerate it. For those students who do enjoy textures, provide a sensory table with sand or liquid soap and water, sandpaper blocks, or smooth stones. The appealing textures will encourage students to handle the objects and therefore use their fine motor skills. (Students can also pour water back and forth in different containers for motor skills practice and get a lesson on volume at the same time.)

- **Small table toys** can be especially appealing and helpful for fine-tuning hand muscles and precision. Many of these, such as plastic frog jumpers, plastic springs, squishy stress balls, and tops are available at dollar stores.

- **Larger toys can be beneficial for fine motor skills.** Dollhouses are good examples. Students have to use a pincer grip to put people in the house and also be precise enough not to knock over other pieces. This can also apply to placing cars on a racetrack or trains on a train track. (If you cannot place a track in your room, laminate a long piece of butcher paper and then use a permanent marker to draw a curvy or zigzag track on the paper. Roll up the track and store it when it is not in use.)

- **Coin Rubbing worksheet (page 23).** Students enjoy playing with coins. Use plastic or real money or tokens and let students do coin rubbings by placing a coin under a sheet of paper and then rubbing over the coin with the side of a crayon until the image appears on top of the paper. If you want to simultaneously teach students the differences between coin values, use the Coin Rubbing worksheet as a homework assignment.

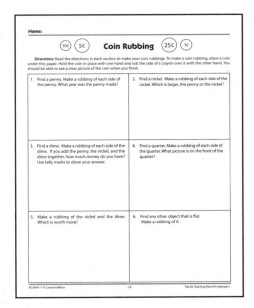

- **Card games are great for fine motor skills** because students have to hold, deal, and shuffle.

- **Video games** are great for developing fine motor skills, and they are often appealing to students with Asperger's.

- **How-to-draw books.** For older elementary students, provide some how-to-draw books in your classroom library. Popular subject matter includes everything from favorite cartoon characters to animals to dinosaurs to princesses!

Make Your Own Paper Airplane

Follow the directions to fold your own airplane.

1. Fold a sheet of plain paper in half. The two long sides should be touching.

2. Open the paper again.

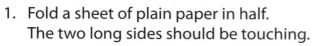

3. Fold the top corners down to touch the crease in the center. They should make two triangles.

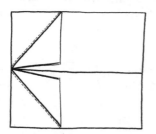

4. Hold the outer edge of one triangle. Fold it in so that it touches the center crease. Fold the edge down.

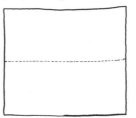

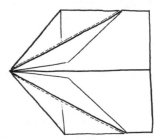

5. Hold the outer edge of the other triangle. Fold it in so that it touches the center crease. Fold the edge down.

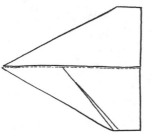

6. Turn the airplane over. Pinch the plane in the middle.

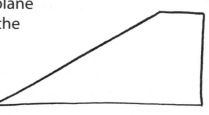

7. Fold one wing over, starting where you are pinching the airplane.

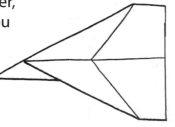

8. Fold the other wing over, starting where you are pinching the airplane. Smooth out the folds so that the creases are sharp.

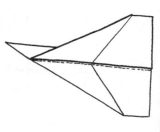

9. Open your wings a little. You are ready to fly your airplane!

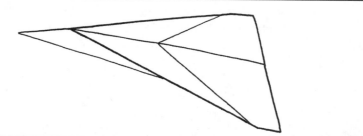

Coin Rubbing

Directions: Read the directions in each section to make your coin rubbings. To make a coin rubbing, place a coin under this paper. Hold the coin in place with one hand and rub the side of a crayon over it with the other hand. You should be able to see a clear picture of the coin when you finish.

1. Find a penny. Make a rubbing of each side of the penny. What year was the penny made?	2. Find a nickel. Make a rubbing of each side of the nickel. Which is larger, the penny or the nickel?
3. Find a dime. Make a rubbing of each side of the dime. If you add the penny, the nickel, and the dime together, how much money do you have? Use tally marks to show your answer.	4. Find a quarter. Make a rubbing of each side of the quarter. What picture is on the front of the quarter?
5. Make a rubbing of the nickel and the dime. Which is worth more?	6. Find any other object that is flat. Make a rubbing of it.

Poor Gross Motor Skills

Students with Asperger's may have an unusual gait and trouble with general coordination. Sports are often difficult, especially those that involve throwing and catching balls. Clumsiness, difficulty with directionality, and general lack of gracefulness can also be typical for these students. While gross motor skills may not directly impact academic success, they are still important for students' confidence, social skills, and overall well-being and health. Students learn teamwork from playing sports, so students who cannot easily participate in team activities at recess miss out on valuable learning experiences and are often frustrated. Students will benefit from these ideas designed to help them overcome difficulties with gross motor skills.

Indicators of Poor Gross Motor Skills

- Falls, trips, or bumps into objects or classmates excessively.

- Walks on tiptoes.

- Seems hesitant when running, navigating stairs, or negotiating through a crowd.

- Makes jerky movements or has a strange gait; arms and legs do not move in a coordinated fashion, and joints seem very stiff. Running or walking seem mechanical or puppet-like.

- Leads with head when walking instead of walking upright.

- When dribbling a basketball, "smacks the ball" (spreads fingers and flattens hand instead of curving it to the shape of the ball); loses control of the ball quickly.

- Unable to clap to a beat or find a rhythm.

Tips and Tricks for Improving Gross Motor Skills

- **Toss soft objects.** Practice throwing and catching with soft objects that do not hurt. Students are braver when catching regular or ball-shaped pillows or squishy balls rather than hard balls. Plus, soft objects do not bounce out of a student's grasp as easily.

- **Workout Routine (page 27).** On days when you cannot get outside, push desks to the side and do some old-fashioned calisthenics that involve large-scale body motions. Consider following a routine like the simple Workout Routine each time. There are several advantages to following a routine. As students learn it, they will become more confident and coordinated by repeating the movements. You can eventually add music to help them feel even more "with it." Or, do the exercises in sets of five or ten to emphasize skip counting along with rhythm.

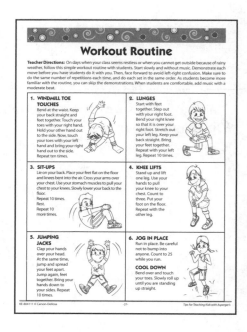

- **Use yoga stretches** as transitions between activities in your classroom. This not only helps students stop one activity and start another; it can help students refocus and provide the student with Asperger's a much-needed opportunity to get some large-muscle stimulation after sitting still for a long time

- **Students love to dance with their teachers!** Because music inspires movement, crank up the tunes and have a dance party in your classroom or take the music outside to give students even more room to move. Kids' music is great, but they will also respond to classical, pop (with appropriate lyrics), or any kind of music you respond to. Be aware of whether this will bother the student with Asperger's; deep bass or loud volume may be hard for the student to handle.

- **Have a rhythm lesson.** Play a song with a slow, definite beat and clap or stomp to it, or march around the room. Do this long enough for every student to find the rhythm. If the student with Asperger's seems unable to match the rhythm with motions, gently take his hands and lead him to clap at the correct intervals. Or, pair students and let them clap together.

- **Plastic hoops are wonderfully creative gross motor tools.** You can have students hop from hoop to hoop, put hoops over their heads and down to the floor, toss balls through them, "hula" with the hoops around waists or arms, roll them and run along beside, spin them on their edges, use them as bases for tag or kickball, etc. Invest in some heavy plastic hoops for your classroom and let students come up with their own ways to play with them.

- **Design an obstacle course** with hoops, ropes, cones, etc. Students will use a variety of gross motor skills to complete it. Instead of making it competitive (and therefore stressful for the student with Asperger's), time each student for two trips through the course and let them try to beat their own personal bests.

- **If you have a student who insists on walking on her tiptoes,** have her stand with her toes on a bottom step and her heels hanging off the edge of the step. Let her relax so that her heels are below her toes to gently stretch her Achilles tendons.

- **If a student has trouble navigating stairs,** line the edge of each step with a strip of masking tape to make stairs look less like ramps. Let the student walk up and down the steps.

- **Competition is stressful.** If you are targeting improving gross motor skills for a student with Asperger's, remember that both competition and cooperation can be very stressful, so keep it separate from gross motor work if you truly want to improve those skills. Activities such as Mother, May I?; Simon Says; and Red Light, Green Light are better than musical chairs or races, where there are clear winners and losers.

- **Mother, May I? is actually a great activity for younger students.** Play this old-fashioned game by giving students directions, such as, "Take two giant steps" or "Take seven mouse steps." Give assignments that are slightly easier for the student with Asperger's. Because every student is likely to forget to say "Mother, May I?" at some point and have to return to the starting line, this game is sillier and less competitive. Instead of designating a winner, just declare the game over when the last student crosses the line so that students are cheering for each other.

- **Freeze tag,** the old favorite where students "freeze" in place when they tag each other until someone tags them out of being frozen, is great for balance and control.

- **Move with Me worksheet (page 28).** It can be helpful for parents to learn how to work on gross motor skills with their children at home. Send home the Move with Me worksheet to give parents some easy ideas.

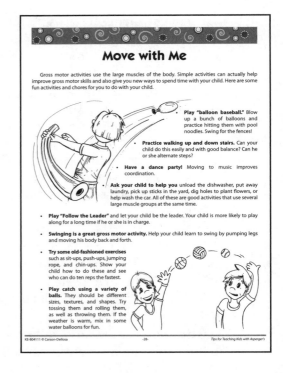

Move with Me

Gross motor activities use the large muscles of the body. Simple activities can actually help improve gross motor skills and also give you new ways to spend time with your child. Here are some fun activities and chores for you to do with your child.

- **Play "balloon baseball."** Blow up a bunch of balloons and practice hitting them with pool noodles. Swing for the fences!

- **Practice walking up and down stairs.** Can your child do this easily and with good balance? Can he or she alternate steps?

- **Have a dance party!** Moving to music improves coordination.

- **Ask your child to help you** unload the dishwasher, put away laundry, pick up sticks in the yard, dig holes to plant flowers, or help wash the car. All of these are good activities that use several large muscle groups at the same time.

- **Play "Follow the Leader"** and let your child be the leader. Your child is more likely to play along for a long time if he or she is in charge.

- **Swinging is a great gross motor activity.** Help your child learn to swing by pumping legs and moving his body back and forth.

- **Try some old-fashioned exercises** such as sit-ups, push-ups, jumping rope, and chin-ups. Show your child how to do these and see who can do ten reps the fastest.

- **Play catch using a variety of balls.** They should be different sizes, textures, and shapes. Try tossing them and rolling them, as well as throwing them. If the weather is warm, mix in some water balloons for fun.

Workout Routine

Teacher Directions: On days when your class seems restless or when you cannot get outside because of rainy weather, follow this simple workout routine with students. Start slowly and without music. Demonstrate each move before you have students do it with you. Then, face forward to avoid left-right confusion. Make sure to do the same number of repetitions each time, and do each set in the same order. As students become more familiar with the routine, you can skip the demonstrations. When students are comfortable, add music with a moderate beat.

1. WINDMILL TOE TOUCHES

Bend at the waist. Keep your back straight and feet together. Touch your toes with your right hand. Hold your other hand out to the side. Now, touch your toes with your left hand and bring your right hand out to the side. Repeat ten times.

2. LUNGES

Start with feet together. Step out with your right foot. Bend your right knee so that it is over your right foot. Stretch out your left leg. Keep your back straight. Bring your feet together. Repeat with your left leg. Repeat 10 times.

3. SIT-UPS

Lie on your back. Place your feet flat on the floor and knees bent into the air. Cross your arms over your chest. Use your stomach muscles to pull your chest to your knees. Slowly lower your back to the floor.
Repeat 10 times.
Rest.
Repeat 10 more times.

4. KNEE LIFTS

Stand up and lift one leg. Use your hands to pull your knee to your chest. Count to three. Put your foot on the floor. Repeat with the other leg.

5. JUMPING JACKS

Clap your hands over your head. At the same time, jump and spread your feet apart. Jump again, feet together. Bring your hands down to your sides. Repeat 10 times.

6. JOG IN PLACE

Run in place. Be careful not to bump into anyone. Count to 25 while you run.

COOL DOWN

Bend over and touch your toes. Slowly roll up until you are standing up straight.

Move with Me

Gross motor activities use the large muscles of the body. Simple activities can actually help improve gross motor skills and also give you new ways to spend time with your child. Here are some fun activities and chores for you to do with your child.

- **Play "balloon baseball."** Blow up a bunch of balloons and practice hitting them with pool noodles. Swing for the fences!

- **Practice walking up and down stairs.** Can your child do this easily and with good balance? Can he or she alternate steps?

- **Have a dance party!** Moving to music improves coordination.

- **Ask your child to help you** unload the dishwasher, put away laundry, pick up sticks in the yard, dig holes to plant flowers, or help wash the car. All of these are good activities that use several large muscle groups at the same time.

- **Play "Follow the Leader"** and let your child be the leader. Your child is more likely to play along for a long time if he or she is in charge.

- **Swinging is a great gross motor activity.** Help your child learn to swing by pumping legs and moving his body back and forth.

- **Try some old-fashioned exercises** such as sit-ups, push-ups, jumping rope, and chin-ups. Show your child how to do these and see who can do ten reps the fastest.

- **Play catch using a variety of balls.** They should be different sizes, textures, and shapes. Try tossing them and rolling them, as well as throwing them. If the weather is warm, mix in some water balloons for fun.

Lack of Spatial Awareness or Difficulty with Directionality

If you have a student who constantly bumps into things and people, she probably lacks spatial awareness. This student may misjudge how her body and other objects fit into surrounding space. She may lack confidence on the playground equipment and when running. She can even be a little dangerous if she is walking or reaching toward another student or handing over scissors, because she cannot stop her forward motion before colliding with her classmate. If you combine this with a lack of directionality, you have a recipe for a student who does not "know where she is in space" on both a small and large scale. While spatial difficulties can be a particular challenge for students with Asperger's-like tendencies, many "typical" students may have this problem because of regular clumsiness or poor vision. These tips will help many students at one time.

Indicators of Lack of Spatial Awareness or Difficulty with Directionality

- Constantly bumps into other students, corners, walls, and tables.

- Falls out of chair or "mis-sits."

- May sit on or against other students when gathering on the floor for story time.

- Bumps into classmates in line or other times when space is not clearly defined; seems to lack peripheral vision as well as depth perception.

- Has a tendency to avoid eye contact, often looks down while walking, and does not have visual reference to keep from bumping into objects.

- Seems nervous or dangerous on playground equipment.

- May have trouble finding his desk, especially after assigned seating has changed.

- Cannot find locations around the school easily or cannot navigate back from destinations; for example, can find the bathroom, but cannot easily return to the classroom.

- When you say, "Raise your right hand," the student guesses, hoping to raise the correct hand.

- Cannot mirror movements; has a hard time mimicking movements when someone is facing him. (Many students and adults have difficulty with this. For a student with Asperger's, trying to mirror movements may almost paralyze her as she tries to figure out which hand to move and how to move it as she tries to "turn" the person she is mimicking in her head.)

Tips and Tricks for Improving Spatial Awareness and Directionality

- **Slow down your transitions.** If students bump into things while moving from one place to another, slow down your transitions. You may lose a little time, but students will arrive less stressed and less bruised.

- **Develop a cue** such as touching a shoulder or saying, "Eyes on me," to remind a student who looks at the floor to look up and make eye contact. This helps in a number of situations, including moving from place to place and making sure the student is listening to directions—especially directions for where to go.

"Eyes on me!"

- **Students with Asperger's have a tendency to avoid eye contact,** so they often look down while walking and then bump into objects and classmates. If a student looks at the floor a lot, mark off frequently used paths with colored masking tape to help guide her around classroom objects such as desk corners.

- **A student who falls out of his chair may do better when seated between two classmates.** Their proximity will make it more difficult for him to misjudge where to sit.

- **Carpet squares.** If students cannot refrain from sitting too close or touching each other while sitting on the floor for story time, tape off sections on the floor or have them sit on carpet squares to enforce each student's own space. Attach the carpet squares with hook-and-loop tape so that they do not slide around.

- **If students sit at tables, use dividers to help them stay in their own spaces.** You can use tape to mark off borders. Or, place a piece of tape in front of each student where you want the center of his body to be when he is sitting.

- **Explore the playground equipment with a student who is nervous about using it** and encourage parents to play on the playground with her after school. She may feel more confident with practice, especially without her classmates watching. Over time, increased muscle and spatial memory will give her more confidence.

- **Use landmarks.** If a student has trouble finding her way by following directions, she may do better using landmarks. Train her to look for different things in the classroom or school building that are recognizable to find her way back. For example, remind her that she sits between Nathan and Diaz, and she should be able to find her seat when she sees them.

- **Reteach position words** because many students do not grasp them well into elementary school. Reinforce your teaching by labeling things in the classroom *left* and *right*, such as the whiteboard. For example, if students say the Pledge of Allegiance, tell them to look at the whiteboard for the symbol that says *right*, and put their right hands over the opposite sides of their chests, because their hearts are always on the left.

- **Play the Hot or Cold game with position words.** Hide something in the classroom and let a few students try to find it. Instead of telling them they are getting warmer, direct them to move left, right, up, or down until they find it.

- **Bring out the "Hokey Pokey" song** to help give students practice with telling left from right.

- **Left and right hands.** Have older students hold up their thumbs and index fingers in the shape of the letter *L*. If it is formed correctly, then they know they are using the correct hand to make it.

- **March left-right-left down the hallway** and help students who seem to march on opposite feet. Do not forget to face away from them as you march; otherwise, they may try to emulate your mirror image.

- **If line spacing is a problem, make a train.** Have each student place one hand at arm's length on the student in front. This is the right space to keep them from bumping into each other.

- **Send the student with Asperger's on errands** or trips to the restroom with a friend at first because he may have a harder time finding his way around the school than most.

- **Maps.** Provide local, city, state, and national maps in your reading center.

- **Prepare a few copies of your school's fire escape routes.** Write the words *Fire Escape* and mark off important landmarks such as your classroom and routes to the office, the cafeteria, the playground, and the closest restroom. Laminate and place them in your reading center for students to read during free time.

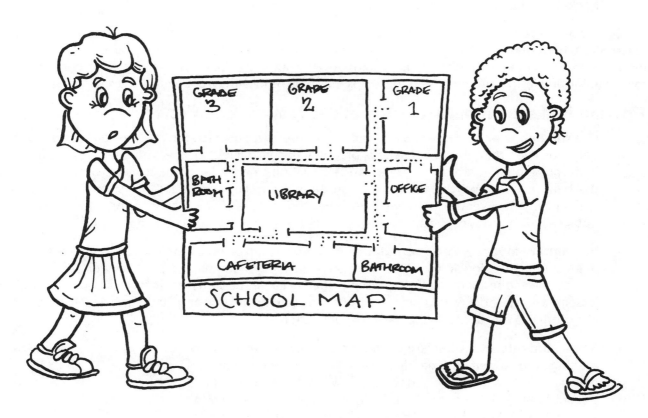

Impulsive or Repetitive Motions and Tics

Some students who have Asperger's syndrome have facial tics or repetitive body motions they cannot control. These can range from winking, to flapping hands, to jerking arms and accidentally hitting other students. Of course, classmates will be upset about being hit, but the student may be very surprised and upset or even angry at being accused of doing it on purpose. It can be very hard to tell the difference between impulsive behavior and uncontrollable actions.

Indicators of Impulsive or Repetitive Motions and Tics

- Makes subtler, habitual motions such as twirling hair or chewing and licking lips.

- Has facial tics and twitches (purses lips, blinks eyes rapidly, shrugs, etc.).

- May have phonic or vocal tics such as tongue clicking, clearing throat, etc.

- Makes repetitive motions (flaps or jerks arms, drums fingers, etc.).

- Rocks back and forth, particularly when in need of comfort.

Obviously, these behaviors are both disruptive and disturbing. After you initially seat the student in a place where she cannot make accidental physical contact with her classmates, work with students to develop their empathy, and acceptance may be the next solution. Here are some ideas for helping these behaviors seem more routine and less disruptive. Using these tips may help reduce the frequency of these behaviors as well.

Tips and Tricks for Impulsive or Repetitive Motions and Tics

- **Use the Behavior Documentation and Action Record Form (page 11)** to record episodes of this behavior. Even though the behavior is probably uncontrollable for the student, using the form may help you record patterns of frequency and intensity. If a particular stimulus seems to start or increase the behavior, you may be able to change the pattern. For example, if the start of the afternoon announcements over the intercom causes the student to lash out with her arms, you may be able to obtain a written copy of the announcements and read them to students instead.

- **Involuntary motion vs. self-stimulation behavior.** It can be hard to tell the difference between a tic or involuntary motion and a self-stimulation behavior. Self-stimulation behaviors, or "self-stims," such as repetitive noises or motions like rocking, often occur as the student attempts to soothe himself and lessen anxiety. Find a way to help the student lessen the anxiety or give the needed stimulation in a less obtrusive way to satisfy the need for stimulation.

- **Some students are not aware of the motions or noises they are making.** You may want to gently point out to the student that he is making a certain motion if you think this will help him control it. If possible, develop a nonverbal cue such as a gentle squeeze on the shoulder to alert the student without calling classmates' attention to the behavior.

- **If you notice that the student's movements or noises increase at certain times of day,** schedule noisier activities during that time so that the self-stim activity is masked by what's going on in the classroom. Use the Behavior Documentation and Action Record Form (page 11) to help you determine the times of day that the activity occurs most.

- **Discover less destructive stimuli.** While the motions or tics may be unavoidable, you may want to try different, less disruptive stimuli, such as stress balls, stretchy bands, chewing gum, or a textured surface to rub her fingers across, to see whether the extra stimulation can reduce some of the motions. Clear any ideas you have with your principal, the student's parents or guardians, and any therapists involved before proceeding.

- **Some students benefit from more "official" stimulus therapies,** such as wearing a weighted vest for deep pressure. Ideas for official therapies usually must have their origin with the student's family or therapist, so document any difficulties the student is having with being able to function in class and submit documentation to the student's therapy team as needed. (If the student is not receiving services, documentation is still a good idea, both for your own records and for the school records, and also in case a diagnosis is given to the student or therapy becomes available.)

- **Be thoughtful about where you seat the student who has very disruptive motions.** He should be seated far enough away from others so that he is less likely to distract or hit classmates and less likely to become embarrassed when making them.

- **Helping classmates understand.** Especially at first, classmates of students who have uncontrollable movements will find extreme examples of this behavior annoying and even upsetting. Handle their complaints with compassion but firmness. Yes, it can be hard to put up with, but if you take it in stride, students are more likely to follow your example and come to see it as part of the daily routine.

- **Classmates will react differently to this behavior.** Some will easily ignore it, while others will let it bother them. Surround the student with sympathetic, mature classmates who can deal with it more easily.

- **Everyone might need a break.** While mainstreaming has many positives, it can occasionally land a highly disruptive and challenging student in your classroom, and it is possible that this student could be one with Asperger's. Sometimes classmates need a break from the student if his behavior is particularly loud or disruptive. If possible, send the student on an errand to the office or allow him to read in the classroom library. Do not call attention to why you are removing him from the classroom. Try to present it like a special treat. You do not want to add hurt feelings to an already tough situation, but if the student with Asperger's is having a challenging day, your other students will appreciate time to regroup, and you may need a breather too. Be sure to send other students on errands as well so that you are not singling out any one student.

High Sensory Needs

Some students with Asperger's have trouble processing sensory information. They may not like loud noises, such as voices and sirens, or background noises, such as the hum of fluorescent lighting. They may not like touch, or they may crave it. They may love or loathe certain smells, textures, or tastes. They may require extra stimulation such as background noise or rocking to get through unpleasant sensory experiences. They may speak with extra-loud voices. You may find out these preferences and needs ahead of time, or you may discover them as they happen in your classroom. Here are some clues to managing different types of sensory needs in your classroom.

Indicators of High Sensory Needs in Students with Asperger's

Because sensory needs are so broad and can differ vastly with each student, it is simplest to cover each sense separately. In all cases, try to make the accommodations as discreet as possible so that the student is not singled out and embarrassed.

Tips and Tricks for Managing High Sensory Needs

Hearing

- **Some students are highly sensitive to loud noises.** If loud voices bother the student, consider allowing him to wear earplugs or headphones that muffle some noise during class discussions or loud activities.

- **Fire alarms.** Alarms upset many students, but since they require exiting the building, you need to keep the student with Asperger's calm enough to do so. Keep a pair of soundproof headphones on a hook near the classroom door. When the fire alarm sounds, give them to this student and help her put them on if necessary. (You can also let her use them for the morning and afternoon announcements if they bother her.) Remind the student that the sooner she leaves the building, the sooner she will be away from the noise.

- **Other students feel frustrated with the constant drone that comes from fluorescent lighting and electronics.** If possible, make sure the student is seated away from the noise. Earplugs and headphones may again be a solution. Or, you could see whether the student can wear a hood or knitted cap during class to give some relief from the buzzing.

- **Other students actually need the constant drone of white noise** because it enables them to focus while tuning out sharper noises. Add a fan or seat the student near a window (to hear passing traffic) or near the computer area to add to the white noise he is able to hear.

Sight

- **If bright light or changing light is a problem,** seat the student away from the windows. If you can configure your seats this way, put her in a corner facing away from the light source. Allow her to wear a hat with a brim.

- **Using an interactive whiteboard with a light-sensitive student** can be helpful because you can dim the light to make the interactive whiteboard more visible. Some students will find comfort in the dim light.

- **Add lamps to your room, open the blinds, and rely less on fluorescent lighting** if it really bothers the student. (See the Classroom Setup section on pages 12–15 for more about lighting and other room decor ideas.)

Smell

- **Most students with Asperger's have an aversion to strong smells** rather than a need for smells. If a cleaning solution or other classroom smell is the problem, that is an easy fix. If it is a classmate whose smell bothers the student, that is a larger issue. If the problem is the classmate's hygiene, then you probably need to speak to the parents, because no student should smell so strongly that it affects others. However, some students do have strong smells, usually because of diet or grooming products. If that is the case, do not seat the two students together, but make it clear that the student with Asperger's is not to be unkind about how his classmate smells.

- **If you do have a student who craves a smell,** allow him to bring in an object with that smell and keep it at his desk, as long as it does not bother another student.

Touch

- **Some students use touch as a self-soothing behavior.** They often want to touch interesting fabric, no matter whom it is on. They may want to rub bumpy concrete walls, or crinkle paper or cellophane, or even push buttons in a vending machine. Self-stim objects that are small enough to bring to class can be noisy and can also encourage others to make noise. Give these students small, quiet substitutes such as sandpaper blocks, beanbags, stress balls or worry stones that can reduce the impulse to touch other things.

- **Set up a classroom sensory table** and fill it with things that meet the need for touching. Make it interesting enough so that other students want to go there during free time too and so the student who truly needs the sensory items stands out less. (This is a preschool trick, but it can also be a soothing and calming influence on older students. If you fill the table with something like rice and add objects related to a science unit, it becomes an extra learning tool.)

- **Hair twirling is a hard habit to break** because hair is always accessible. If the student likes to twirl her own hair, ask parents to pull her hair back or suggest cutting it shorter so that it is not a distraction.

- **Touching others.** Some students' need for touch, combined with their impulsiveness, will lead to them touching others. For example, a student who likes to twirl her own hair will probably want to twirl the long, curly hair of the student in front of her. The student who needs to rub sandpaper will want to rub the plastic, printed figures on his friend's superhero T–shirt. It is usually best just to remove the temptation. However, if a student cannot keep his hands to himself, seat him out of reach from other classmates. Put him at the front of the line so that there is no one in front of him to touch.

- **Inappropriate touching.** Occasionally, students will decide to touch their bodies in inappropriate places. While this is common and not that big of a deal in very young students, it becomes highly inappropriate with older elementary students. It is a good idea to talk to parents and let them know that it is not OK for their child to do this at school, in case they are letting it happen at home. You can state that it will cause classmates to ask questions neither you nor the student should have to answer. When it happens, it is fine to tell the student that this kind of touching is for private time. Develop a silent cue with the student such as a pat on the arm or shoulder, to let him know to stop the touching. The cue needs to be a silent, touching cue because many times the student will not make eye contact, and because everyone in the class will turn around to see what that student is doing if you call the student's name.

- **Highly sensitive or insensitive to touch.** Sometimes, a student with Asperger's dislikes touching altogether or is highly sensitive to it. Itchy clothing, tags, or buttons may bother this student and cause him to act out constantly. Conversely, the student may be insensitive or unresponsive to pain or to hot or cold temperatures, which can be dangerous. Any issues like these should lead you straight to parents or an occupational therapist, as these issues will be too challenging to deal with on your own.

Taste and Other Food Issues

Along with other sensory needs, food can be another area of sensitivity with students with Asperger's. They may have significant food preferences and strong aversions, and also motor skill and muscle control issues that cause difficulty with chewing and swallowing. You should be aware of these in case a homemade lunch is forgotten, there is a class party, or you eat out on a field trip. Students with Asperger's may prefer a bland diet that is limited to a few particular tastes or textures. Be prepared to work with parents, many of whom will have been coached by pediatricians to try to broaden their children's food preferences for nutritional reasons.

Indicators of Food Issues

- Has a very limited diet, may only eat a few foods, and prefers only a few brands.

- May have unusual ways of eating foods.

- Sensory issues may spill over into a student's eating habits. Things such as a low tolerance for loud lunchrooms, issues with textures, or even preferences for very bland food may dictate what a student is willing to eat.

- Even if the student is not picky about her own food, others' food choices may bother her.

- A need for rituals may also affect a student's eating habits. If a student brings the same food each day, she may become upset and unable to continue her lunch if something is missing or if it is in different containers than what she is used to. (See more about rituals below and on page 38.)

Tips and Tricks for Managing Food Issues

- **Limited food choices.** Students with Asperger's often do not eat a lot of food, although there are always exceptions. They may also limit their diets to very few food choices and may tend to choose unhealthful foods. If this is the case and you are truly concerned about a student's diet, discuss the issue with your school's guidance counselor and principal. This is a parenting issue, and your recourse may be very limited, especially if some of the dietary limitations are caused by medications. Know what you are and are not allowed to say and do according to your school's policies before you speak with parents.

- **Food wrappers.** Students may be sensitive about what their foods are packaged in. For example, they may not like the smell of plastic bags and insist that their sandwiches be packed in waxed paper. Or, they may not like the sound or the feel of unwrapping foil. If you notice a difference in how much the student is willing to eat based on how her lunch is packaged, talk with the student to see if you can determine what the issues are. Share your observations with parents. When it is reasonable, encourage the student to return the uneaten portion of food in her lunch box so that her parents will know what she has and has not eaten.

- **Emergency food.** Where food comes from can be as important as what the food is. The student may have a hard time eating unfamiliar food even if it is essentially the same thing. For example, if a student forgets his peanut butter sandwich, and you offer to make him one in the staff room, he may turn you down because the bread and peanut butter are different brands, or even just because they are not from home. Ask parents to bring in a few prepackaged items the student will certainly eat and store them in the classroom in case of emergency.

- **If a student has unusual eating habits,** allow the habits unless they cause disruption at the lunch table. For example, a student who eats her pudding with a fork is not a problem. A student who prefers slurping her pudding with a straw is a bit problematic, and you may need to insist that she eat it with a spoon or bring another dessert.

- **Food rituals.** A ritual is a repetitive behavior that must happen for the student to feel comfortable doing the activity. Students with Asperger's may have rituals that revolve around food. For example, a student may need to eat the same foods every day in the same order to get through lunch smoothly. As long as parents remember to pack blueberries, crackers, a ham sandwich, and milk every day, in the same containers, then lunch will not be a problem. However, on the days when parents forget or substitute an item, or put the blueberries in the yellow container instead of the green one, the student may be upset. At this point, you cannot make the green container magically appear, so offer her a choice between eating the blueberries or skipping that part of her lunch. Let her choose between just two or three options so that you do not endlessly negotiate with her.

- **Pack his own lunch.** If the student is older, suggest to parents that he be in charge of packing his own lunch. This way, he can decide what containers and items he is comfortable with and can be responsible for what reaction he will have when he opens his lunch the next day.

- **Lunchtime routines.** Going to the cafeteria may be like any other special activity and may be perceived as an interruption to the safe and familiar classroom routine. Consider establishing routines by giving assigned seating, taking the same route each day, or making other modifications to help the student learn to consider taking this trip as part of her everyday routine.

- **School cafeterias are very noisy places** when packed full of students. If the problem is that the cafeteria is too noisy, let the student wear earplugs or ask if your class can be seated in a less crowded area where the student may be more comfortable.

- **Lunchtime Contract (page 39).** For a student who disrupts lunchtime for others because of her eating habits or rituals, you may need to make a contract. Use the Lunchtime Contract to write up a short list of agreements between you and the student about what is and is not acceptable behavior at lunchtime. Tailor it to the student's needs. Both of you should sign it and then review it before lunch each day until she is following it without reminders. Be sure to keep your end of the bargain—the reward end!

# Lunchtime Contract

Student's Name: _____ Date: _____

Teacher's Name: _____

I want to have a good lunch! I want my friends to enjoy their lunches too!
Here are some things I can do to help make this happen.

1. _____

2. _____

3. _____

4. _____

Rewards for following lunchtime contract agreements after five days: _____

_____

Consequences for breaking lunchtime contract agreements more than once in five days:

_____

Student's signature: _____ Date:_____

Teacher's signature: _____ Date:_____

Parent's signature: _____ Date: _____

Language and Literacy

Students with Asperger's syndrome frequently come to class with language skills at grade level or higher. However, their style of speech and choice of topics can be markedly different from those of their classmates, making it hard for other students to warm up to them through conversations. Students with Asperger's may have excellent vocabularies and extensive knowledge about their favorite subjects, yet be reluctant to talk much outside of the subject areas. They may chat with classmates quite a bit but seem unaware or unconcerned with whether their classmates are interested or even listening to them. Their prosody (stress, intonation, and rhythm of their speech) may be strange and inappropriate. When reading, their ability to engage with fiction may also be impaired.

Fortunately, it is possible to teach students with Asperger's to listen to themselves and to observe others around them to pick up cues about how to successfully communicate. Learning to self-monitor can be difficult for young students, but if they start trying to have successful conversations at an early age, it can get easier as time goes on. These skills, combined with those in the next section (Social and Emotional Development, page 60), can help students look for cues that will help them develop conversational skills that are appropriate in formal classroom settings, as well as in social settings.

Limited Receptive Language Skills

By late preschool and early elementary school, many students with Asperger's have acquired age-appropriate expressive language as far as vocabulary and sentence structure. By grades K–2, they can express their needs, speak clearly and in complete sentences, and have sufficient or even exceptional vocabularies. In other words, a language delay will not usually be a problem for a student with Asperger's. (There are always exceptions to this rule.)

However, while a student may exhibit plenty of expressive language, a delay in receptive language is something to look out for. Teachers often think that when a highly verbal student with Asperger's-like behaviors has trouble following directions or completing assignments, he has not been paying attention. But, it may be a mistake to assume that because the student talks well, he can understand things equally well. He may instead be very literal and not understand everything others say, or be unable to organize or process information well. Therefore, use these suggestions to check the student's understanding often.

Indicators of Limited Receptive Language Skills

- Does not look as though he understands; gives you a blank look after you speak.

- Completes assignments or follows simple directions incorrectly.

- Answers simple questions incorrectly.

- Cannot repeat things back to you completely or in the right order.

Tips and Tricks for Managing Limited Receptive Language

- **Notice whether a student understands you through her work**—if her work is wrong, go back over it, making an assumption that she did not understand. Do not jump to the conclusion that the student did not pay attention.

- **Have the student repeat things back to you,** especially multiple-step directions.

- **Make sure you have more explicit written directions, along with pictures or examples, for a student with Asperger's.** For example, if you are making a craft, you may need to add extra details to the directions for this student or break down directions into shorter, simpler steps. Also, show the craft at various stages of completion.

- **Revisit each step** to make sure it is completed properly before moving to the next one. That way, you avoid having to backtrack so much when something goes wrong.

- **Be more creative and specific about how you ask whether students understand.** For example, when you say, "Add details to the picture," ask, "Do you understand what I mean by add details? Give me an example of a detail you want to add." If the student says, "I want to put stripes on the cat," you know the student understands what a detail is. If the student says, "I want to put a tail on the cat," this is wrong because most cats have tails, so it is not a detail.

- **When you ask a question, ask it with a short sentence and build in plenty of wait time for the student to answer.** It may take more time for a student with Asperger's to process what you say and therefore more time to answer your questions, so slow down and wait patiently.

- **Be patient if the student interrupts you frequently.** Point out her interruptions because she may not be aware of them, but also realize that she may not know she is doing it, and it may be a crucial part of her attempt to process what you are saying.

- **Use the Catch You Later! Let's Learn Some Idioms worksheet (page 43).** Idioms are an important part of everyday speech, but when you use them, follow up with literal explanations of what you are "really" saying. For example, if you say it is time to "hit the books" when it is time to get to work, you may need to explain that you mean it is time to work hard at something. Use the Catch You Later! Let's Learn Some Idioms worksheet to help students learn some common figures of speech.

- **Offer the same kinds of explanations with slang, jokes, humorous sarcasm, silly comments from other students, and even tone.** Mediate conversations between classmates if there are misunderstandings between friends. For example, if a student takes what a classmate says literally, you may have to soothe hurt feelings and do some interpreting.

- **Check facial expressions.** Expressions can tell you a lot without saying a word, even though students with Asperger's sometimes have trouble reading facial expressions on others' faces. The student can look confused, frustrated, or tuned out when she does not grasp what you are saying, just like any other student.

- **Do not check in with just one student when you are trying to gauge understanding in your classroom.** It is likely that other students do not understand parts of your lesson as well. The student with Asperger's does not always need to be the one who is singled out. Plus, hearing it explained to another student can add to their understanding. Ask three or four students to explain what they think you mean so that the whole class hears it expressed in several ways, and you get a chance to reword things. You may find out that your clear directions are not so clear after all.

- **Finally, give students tools to tell you they do not understand.** Make a list of standard questions they can ask you and come up with a system for them to use to signal you that they are lost. For example, color one side of an index card green and the other red. Ask the student to show the green side of the card on his desk when he is comfortable with the work he is doing, and flip it to the red side when he is confused.

Name: _____

Catch You Later! Let's Learn Some Idioms

Directions: Read the phrases below. Write what you think they really mean.
Listen as your teacher talks about them. On the back of the paper, draw a picture of your favorite.

1. That dripping noise drives me up the wall. _____
_____

2. Your dad will hit the roof when he finds out you broke the window. _____
_____

3. Count on me to be there. _____
_____

4. It's time to go. Let's roll! _____
_____

5. Pizza? I am all over that! _____
_____

6. My sister blew up when I borrowed her bike without asking. _____
_____

7. It is not going to rain tonight! Bite your tongue! _____
_____

8. When my mom is angry, I walk on eggshells at my house. _____
_____

Random Speech, Comfort Speech, Echolalia

Just like some students twirl their hair or drum their fingers to comfort themselves, some students on the Autism spectrum use comfort speech to make themselves feel better. This can be an interim step in the process of developing language skills. It can also be a way to deal with something that is difficult or frightening, or it can work its way into being a habit.

Random speech and comfort speech mean repeated words that do not seem related to the situation, at least not content-wise. Usually, the trigger for it is contained in the situation. For example, if a student repeats a seemingly random phrase to himself when he is tense or upset, even though it seems to have very little to do with what is going on around him at the moment, this is probably comfort speech.

Echolalia is repeating speech that another person has recently spoken in a conversation. The student may repeat things heard just moments ago in class, but then may repeat them later on as well. Hearing your words come right back at you can break your concentration as a teacher and can give classmates the impression that the student is copying them, which is something students do intentionally to annoy each other.

Both kinds of speech can be helpful to a student with Asperger's because they each serve a purpose, but they can be distracting to classmates. Here are signs that a student is using these types of speech for comfort or for other reasons.

Indicators of Random Speech, Comfort Speech, and Echolalia

*   Repeats random noises, words, phrases, or songs.

*   Says things that frequently seem out of context.

*   Seems to have a trigger—a time of day, location, or even an activity that causes random speech to break out.

*   Is compelled to repeat after the teacher, even when asked not to do so.

*   Repeats snippets of others' conversations, even when it clearly bothers classmates.

*   May get stuck in a sentence and repeat a few words several times before being able to complete a thought.

*   Exhibits echolalia by repeating what you or other students say just after hearing it, which sounds like mocking.

Tips and Tricks for Managing Random Speech, Comfort Speech, and Echolalia

*   Keep notes about when the random speech or comfort speech occurs so that you can try to spot patterns. If you can track times or places that the speech shows up, then you can figure out what stresses may be causing it and try to lessen them.

- **Ask the student why she needs to repeat those words every day.** Older students may be able to tell you. They may even be able to tell you how to change the day so they do not have to say them. For example, maybe the student does not like to go into the loud, echoing bathroom after lunch, and it makes her talk to herself to lessen the stress. If this is the case, you can send her into a smaller bathroom that does not cause so much stress, and you can strike a bargain with her to reduce the comfort speech as a result.

- **When you do something to help a student reduce comfort speech, remind him that you are not punishing him for using it.** Instead, you have tried to help him be less stressed so that he does not have to use it. Remember, though, that comforting themselves is something all students do, just in less obvious ways. Maintain your patience with the student as he tries to reduce the behavior, and remember, it is not something that will necessarily go away completely.

- **Echolalia can be developmental.** Repeating what people say can help students internalize directions or information as they learn it. If you have a student who is at that developmental level, normalize the behavior by having other students repeat directions so that the student with Asperger's does not stand out.

- **Repeat both the question and the answer.** If you ask a question and then supply an answer, have students repeat both the question and the answer so that they are voicing both. For example, if you say, "What is this flower? It is a daisy," have them repeat, "What is this flower? It is a daisy." This way, they are learning all of the information, not just the answer. This is another way to have them normalize the behavior, especially if you do it rhythmically.

- **Explain to classmates that the student who echoes is not "copying them."** She is using their language to learn. When students understand that, they are likely to be much more patient and kind.

- **Talking out loud during tests.** When classmates are learning independently or taking tests, it can be very distracting to have a student randomly speaking during quiet times. Try to seat this student a little distance away from others to give them a less distracting testing experience. If the student's speech is very loud during testing, you may need to apply to get that student accommodations for separate testing.

- **Talking out loud.** We all talk to ourselves, but most of us do not do it out loud. Work with students who have not learned to internalize their speech. Help them learn to think to themselves instead of thinking out loud and to learn to monitor their volume and speak as quietly to themselves as possible. If they can learn to control their volume while talking to themselves, this can make a huge difference in your class's comfort level. Whispering is less distracting than talking.

- **Referral to a Speech Therapist.** Students may be eligible to work with speech therapists if they have severe echolalia; speech therapy eligibility may come before an Asperger's diagnosis. If this is not the case in your district, and echolalia is impairing learning, consider starting the process for a speech therapist referral.

Perseveration (Obsession with One Subject)

We all have favorite topics: things that we know a lot about and that we are comfortable talking about. If someone introduces that favorite topic, it does not take much for us to chime in on it. What sets students with Asperger's apart from most people is that, if they are given even the tiniest opening into a favorite topic, they can be perfectly oblivious to others' attempts at contributing to the conversation, or to changing the subject. Other people become merely the audience for everything you ever wanted to know about cars, trains, elephants, or whatever the topic is. Objects with motion, such as tornadoes and racetracks, are popular subject matters, as are things with statistics, such as sports and weather. For slightly older students, certain topics such as popular books or trading cards can be big attractions. Knowing this much information about one topic is not a bad thing—except when talking about it all the time takes the place of having normal conversations with friends or class discussions about school subjects.

Indicators of Perseveration

- Possesses a wealth of information about a topic than is far more in-depth than what most children this age usually have.

- Introduces the favorite topic at random, even when no one else is talking about it.

- Attempts to bring conversations around to this topic at any cost, even if it seems awkward.

- Recites random statistics about this topic.

- Ignores reactions and social cues by others involved in the conversation, such as trying to change the topic or trying to excuse themselves.

- Takes over classroom discussions about school-related topics to inject comments about the favorite topic.

- Adults' reactions to the information overload are usually to think that this student is "smart" or "quirky," so they can unwittingly encourage the behavior.

- Free-choice artwork, book selections, and writing assignments all revolve around the favorite topic.

Tips and Tricks for Managing Perseveration

- **Be gentle but direct when discussing perseveration.** This is not the time for subtle hints. Some students will be self-aware enough to know that their conversations do not seem to work like other students' do and will already be clued in that some of their classmates do not seem to enjoy talking to them for very long. Offer suggestions (such as those listed here and in the Inability to Start or Join a Conversation section on page 82) for how they can connect more easily by not talking about the same thing all of the time.

- **Let's Talk! worksheet (page 50).** Use examples to show the student how most people have conversations. Use the Let's Talk worksheet to give some examples for how people talk to each other and then let the student work with you to write his own.

- **Stay on the original topic.** Put this in a classroom context. When you ask a question in the classroom, and the student starts straying off topic, steer her back to the original topic or move to another student. The longer her discussion stays relevant to the topic at hand, the longer she will get to contribute.

- **Conversation Rules for Kids worksheet (page 51).** Explain that there are rules most people follow when they have conversations. People move from topic to topic instead of talking about the same thing for a very long time. They pause after they say things and wait for others to speak. They ask questions and answer them when asked. Read the Conversation Rules for Kids worksheet and discuss these rules as a class or in small groups. If you use small groups, try to have an adult monitor each one. Or, invite your school guidance counselor to help you with this activity. (This worksheet is good practice for reading and writing conversations as well.)

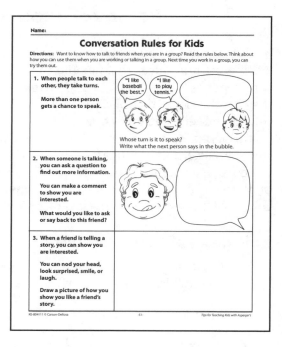

- **Role-play with the student to show her how to answer questions in class.** For example, ask a question and then give her the answer. Have her raise her hand and give the answer back to you. Do this activity with the entire class so that everyone has extra examples to follow. For example, if the student tends to elaborate, and you ask a question that just needs a short answer, such as "What is the weather like outside today," say, "Look, it's sunny and warm!" Have the student repeat your answer. To make it more challenging for older students, ask how they can give the same answer with different words but still keep it short.

- **Break students into small discussion groups and assign conversation topics.** Explain that they are responsible for staying on topic and talking for a given length of time. Adjust the time according to how old they are and make sure the topics will interest them, but steer clear of the topic that causes the student with Asperger's to perseverate. Choose topics that the other students will find interesting and have in common so that they can keep things moving in the conversation. Let them discuss a recent field trip, what everyone brought for lunch that day, whether they like the class book you are reading, or any other topic students can all contribute to.

- **Signals for transitioning.** If the student does get going on his favorite topic, work with him to come up with some cues for when it is time to let it go. You can touch him on the arm or shoulder and say, "Thank you for telling us that, Alex," ring a bell that signals other transitions, or use any other cue that you and the student agree on that works. It can be hard to stop the flow once it starts, so you may need to try a few things to see what interrupts the flow.

- **Try to let the student's need to indulge in this topic be met in other ways such as through drawing, reading, or writing.** Talking and learning about the favorite topic fulfills a need for this student, so trying to shut it down completely is not necessarily a good idea. The point is to steer the conversation away from it so it does not get in the way of classroom activity and normal conversations. If the student is able to find an outlet for his train fixation through drawing pictures of trains, reading about them, and writing train stories, then he may feel less compelled to talk nonstop about them.

- **Encourage more than one topic.** Although you do want the student to indulge in her favorite topic in other ways to avoid talking about it too much, do not let her indulge in this topic as therapy forever. You do not want her to repeat the same reading over and over in place of talking about it. Keep track of the student's book and art selections. If a student constantly checks out the same books, assign additional books with different topics to broaden her horizons. Do the same thing with writing and art assignments. If you usually give free writing assignments, and you notice that the student constantly writes about the same thing, make sure to give additional assignments so that there is variety in the student's work. Explain that you are interested in how she feels about other things besides that one topic and that you want to read about that in her writing too.

Let's Talk!

Directions: Read what the first person says in each picture.
Draw a speech bubble around what you think the second person should say.

Answer 1.
No, thanks. I want to play soccer with Kim.

Answer 2.
My favorite game is football.

Answer 1.
Sure, here it is.

Answer 2.
You didn't say please! You broke the rules!

Answer 1.
I like art, Miss Simpson.

Answer 2.
I drew my family. This is my sister and my big brother and my mom.

Answer 1.
I ride on bus number 7. I like the number 7. I have a number 7 shirt.

Answer 2.
Yes, I ride with Malik every Tuesday. What bus do you ride?

Conversation Rules for Kids

Directions: Want to know how to talk to friends when you are in a group? Read the rules below. Think about how you can use them when you are working or talking in a group. Next time you work in a group, you can try them out.

1. **When people talk to each other, they take turns.** **More than one person gets a chance to speak.**	 "I like baseball the best." "I like to play tennis." Whose turn is it to speak? Write what the next person says in the bubble.
2. **When someone is talking, you can ask a question to find out more information.** **You can make a comment to show you are interested.** **What would you like to ask or say back to this friend?**	
3. **When a friend is telling a story, you can show you are interested.** **You can nod your head, look surprised, smile, or laugh.** **Draw a picture of how you show you like a friend's story.**	

Difficulty with Reading and Writing Fiction

Students with Asperger's often have a hard time with make-believe and pretend play, so of course they tend to prefer reading nonfiction and statistics to fiction. This limits their ability to gain understanding of social interaction that is present in many works of fiction and also can hurt their critical thinking and writing skills. It may be hard to find fiction that suits them, but it's worth the hard work because they will benefit in so many ways, including improved social skills. Use these ideas to find fiction that works for students with Asperger's.

Indicators of Difficulty with Reading and Writing Fiction

- Checks nonfiction books out of the library and either avoids stories altogether or checks out the same ones. (These may be way below grade level.)

- Struggles with retelling fictional stories, especially with explaining why things happened.

- Cannot give the main idea in a story; instead, gives random details but not the big picture.

- Cannot understand figurative language or assign meaning to it.

- Cannot answer comprehension questions, such as, "Why did the author write this story?" Also has trouble with cause and effect, making inferences, and drawing conclusions.

- Cannot distinguish between fact and opinion; tends to think everything is a fact, except for opinions he disagrees with.

- Tends to translate difficulties with reading comprehension to writing; may have difficulty with storytelling in writing; stories often do not have a point or do not relate to the assigned topic or prompt.

- When writing an assignment for an audience other than the teacher, such as a note to a classmate or a thank-you note, cannot imagine how to write to a different audience.

Tips and Tricks for Managing a Student's Difficulty with Reading and Writing Fiction

- **Find a book series that works.** Certain fiction works better for students with Asperger's. For example, many students with Asperger's like series because they like to get through the numbered books. Introduce the starter book for several series until you find one that "clicks."

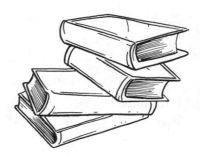

- **Science fiction can work well as reading material because it is full of new and creative things to memorize.** Science fiction offers a lot of facts to learn, such as new technology, different races, new creatures, and new vocabulary, that captivate plenty of students and gives them all something in common to discuss.

- **Fact or Opinion? worksheet (page 55).** Do a "fact or opinion" shout out for students who have trouble telling the difference between the two. Say something that is clearly opinion such as, "Chocolate chip cookies are the best cookies!" Or, try a fact such as, "There are many rocks in the ground." Let students raise their hands and say whether they think it is fact or opinion and then say why. For further practice, send home the Fact or Opinion? worksheet and ask students to complete it with parents.

- **The Main Idea worksheet (page 56).** Sometimes, students weigh all information as being of the same importance. This worksheet helps teach them not to. Read the passages with students and talk about which answer seems to be the main idea and why.

- **The Make an Inference worksheet (page 57)** tests how well students gather implied information and apply it to come up with logical conclusions. After doing this worksheet as a whole class or in small groups, read a short story and pause at different places to ask a few students what they think will happen next.

- **The Sequence of Events worksheet (page 58)** is similar to the Make an Inference worksheet in that students are dealing with what happens next, except that students already have all of the events in hand. In this case, they have to figure out the order in which events occurred.

- **The Character Study worksheet (page 59)** helps students learn about a character and can be used with characters in books and for older elementary students with stories they want to write.

- **As students learn to read literature, they need to be able to make connections to their own lives to make their reading more meaningful.** This is a fairly abstract task for younger students anyway, but for students with Asperger's, who tend to be very literal, making a connection that is not exactly like the book can be very tough. Point out similarities such as, "In both stories, the animals can talk," or, "The main character loves her dog, and you love your pet too."

- **Another challenge for students with Asperger's is for them to tell why they think the author wrote an article or story.** Is its purpose to entertain? To teach a lesson? To teach facts about something? Work with students to help them understand what the purpose of a piece of writing might be. For example, if you read an article about frogs, they should be able to understand that the author wrote the article to tell facts about frogs. Practice with nonfiction pieces first because the author's purpose is easier to determine.

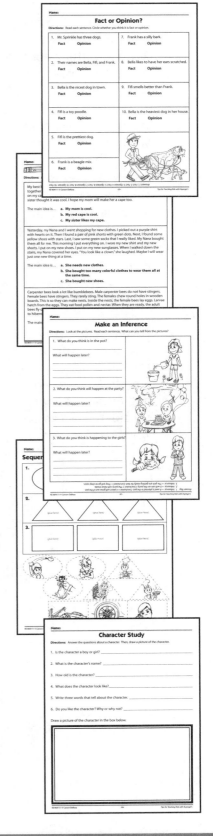

- **Students with Asperger's may have trouble reading personal narratives.** To get around this, ask the student if she were the one doing the writing, what would she want students to know? Then, ask her to think about what the author might want her to know. How can she find this out from the writing? It is hard for the student to put herself in someone else's shoes, but thinking about it from her point of view first may be helpful.

- **Write more content.** When you have one-on-one writing sessions with these students, help them work on elaborating, both to give more information and to help them write longer sentences.

- **Learn to recognize when "enough is enough."** On the other hand, if you have a student with Asperger's that talks for long periods of time about favorite topics, this habit may translate into writing sentences that are pages long. Help these students learn that it is fine to add periods and other punctuation and to limit themselves to one or two thoughts per sentence.

- **Often, student writers focus on minute details and leave out action and meaning.** Work with them to balance these areas. Ask questions that will get students to add more important information, not more extraneous details. This helps students consider what the audience is interested in learning, which is an important step for a writer of any age.

Name:

Fact or Opinion?

Directions: Read each sentence. Circle whether you think it is fact or opinion.

1. Mr. Sprinkle has three dogs. **Fact** **Opinion**	7. Frank has a silly bark. **Fact** **Opinion**
2. Their names are Bella, Fifi, and Frank. **Fact** **Opinion**	8. Bella likes to have her ears scratched. **Fact** **Opinion**
3. Bella is the nicest dog in town. **Fact** **Opinion**	9. Fifi smells better than Frank. **Fact** **Opinion**
4. Fifi is a toy poodle. **Fact** **Opinion**	10. Bella is the heaviest dog in her house. **Fact** **Opinion**
5. Fifi is the prettiest dog. **Fact** **Opinion**	
6. Frank is a beagle mix. **Fact** **Opinion**	

Answers: 1. Fact 2. Fact 3. Opinion 4. Fact 5. Opinion 6. Fact 7. Opinion 8. Fact 9. Opinion 10. Fact

 # Main Idea

Directions: Read each paragraph. Circle each main idea.

My best birthday present was a red cape. My mom made it out of red fabric. She tied it together under my neck and told me I was a superhero. Then, she painted a big letter *S* on my cape. I looked so cool! I pretended to fly around the house all day. Even my big sister thought it was cool. I hope my mom will make her a cape too.

The main idea is…
    a. My mom is cool.
    b. My red cape is cool.
    c. My sister likes my cape.

Yesterday, my Nana and I went shopping for new clothes. I picked out a purple shirt with hearts on it. Then, I found a pair of pink shorts with green dots. Next, I found some yellow shoes with stars. Last, I saw some green socks that I really liked. My Nana bought them all for me. This morning, I put everything on. I wore my new shirt and my new shorts. I put on my new shoes. I put on my new sunglasses. When I walked down the stairs, my Nana covered her eyes. "You look like a clown," she laughed. Maybe I will wear just one new thing at a time.

The main idea is…
    a. She needs new clothes.
    b. She bought too many colorful clothes to wear them all at the same time.
    c. She bought new shoes.

Carpenter bees look a lot like bumblebees. Male carpenter bees do not have stingers. Female bees have stingers. They rarely sting. The females chew round holes in wooden boards. This is so they can make nests. Inside the nests, the female bees lay eggs. Larvae hatch from the eggs. They eat food pollen and nectar. When they are ready, the adult bees fly out in late summer. They pollinate flowers and gather food. Then, they get ready to hibernate until spring.

The main idea is…
    a. Carpenter bees gather food.
    b. Carpenter bees hibernate.
    c. These are facts about carpenter bees.

Name:

Make an Inference

Directions: Look at the pictures. Read each sentence. What can you tell from the pictures?

1. What do you think is in the pot?

____

What will happen later?

____

____

____

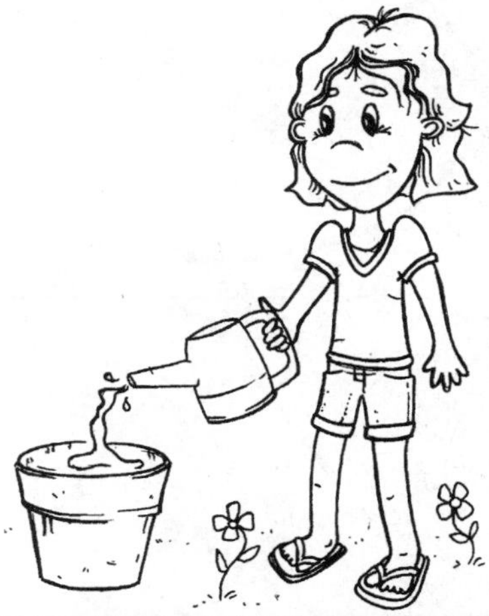

2. What do you think will happen at the party?

____

What will happen later?

____

____

____

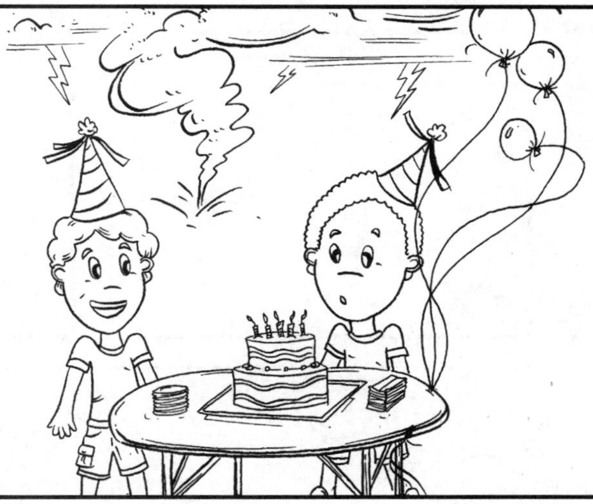

3. What do you think is happening to the girls?

____

What will happen later?

____

____

____

Answer Key: 1. Inference = A seed is planted in the pot. Conclusion = A plant will grow out of the pot.
2. Inference = It will rain on the party. Conclusion = The party will move inside.
3. Inference = The girls are getting ready for bed. Conclusion = They will go to sleep soon.

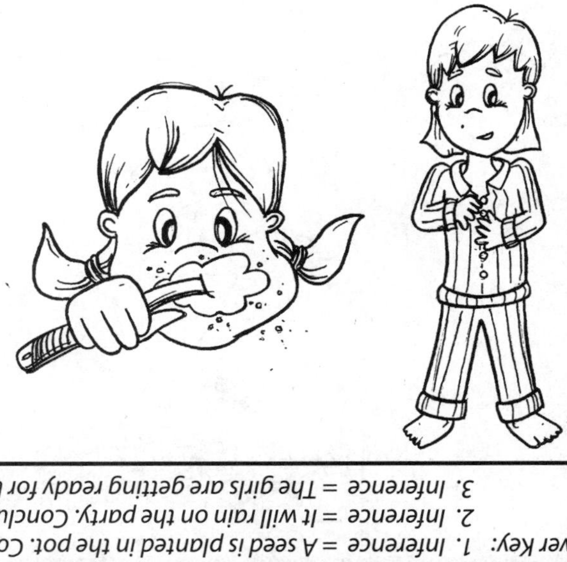

Name:

Sequence of Events

Directions: Cut out the pictures at the bottom of the page. Glue them in the correct order in the matching shapes at the top of the page.

1.

(glue here)   (glue here)   (glue here)

2.

(glue here)   (glue here)   (glue here)

3.

(glue here)   (glue here)   (glue here)

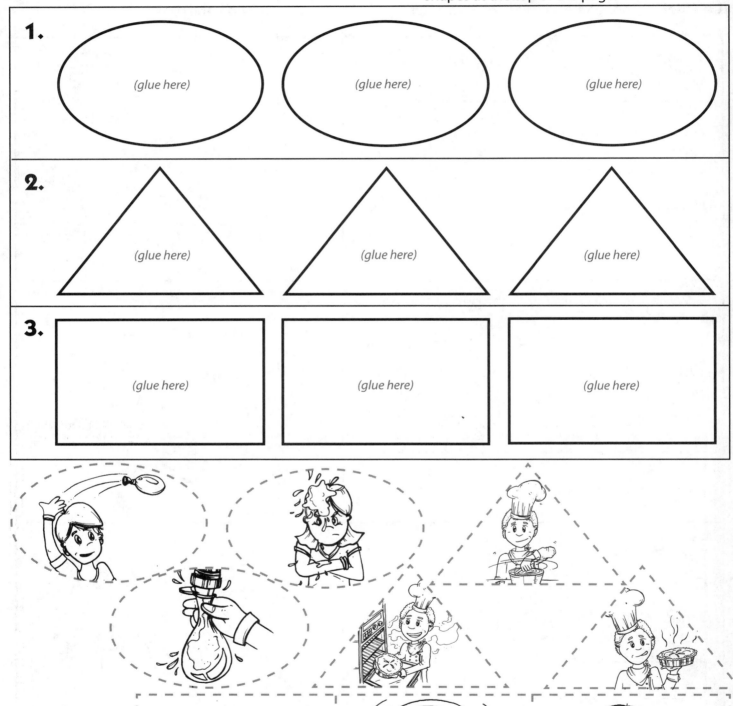

-58- *Tips for Teaching Kids with Asperger's*

Character Study

Directions: Answer the questions about a character. Then, draw a picture of the character.

1. Is the character a boy or girl? _____

2. What is the character's name? _____

3. How old is the character? _____

4. What does the character look like? _____

5. Write three words that tell about the character. _____

6. Do you like the character? Why or why not? _____

Draw a picture of the character in the box below.

Social and Emotional Development

Social skills are not a graded part of most academic curriculums. However, many factors in the current elementary school environment have made it necessary for teachers to focus on the social behavior of their students. Anti-bullying programs in many schools introduce students to how they should not treat each other. Student behavior in the classroom is an ever-present dynamic that teachers must manage. And, teachers are expected to do less individual teaching and more group facilitating, supposedly to emulate students' future teamwork environments in the workplace. If you add a student with Asperger's to this mix, you have an even higher likelihood of needing to address social skills.

Typically, students with Asperger's have a hard time picking up on social cues and developing friendships. They are likely to need support and coaching in this area. Although your primary job is to make sure this student reaches grade-appropriate academic goals, implementing the ideas on pages 61–62 can help the student learn to understand how classmates interact and can help her make friends and navigate difficult social situations. Involve your principal or director, school guidance counselor, and parents as appropriate if any situations arise between this student and classmates that are to difficult to deal with in the classroom setting. And, be sure to document any instances of bullying in detail.

Finally, note that there are three very similar discussions in this book: Lack of Spatial Awareness or Difficulty with Directionality (page 29), Lack of Respect for Personal Space (page 61), and Inappropriate Physical Contact (Others and Self) (page 63). The first, Lack of Spatial Awareness or Difficulty with Directionality, refers to students who do not have a clear awareness of where their bodies end and others' bodies (or walls, corners, or any other objects) begin. The second, Lack of Respect for Personal Space, deals with students who do not understand that classmates do not like to be inches from their friends, but rather about an arm's length. The third, Inappropriate Physical Contact, deals more with how and when students should touch each other and themselves. There is some overlap in these topics, but they are three separate issues and therefore are dealt with separately.

Lack of Respect for Personal Space

Students with Asperger's sometimes have a tough time knowing how close is too close. A student may get right in the face of a classmate to have a normal conversation. Because volume control can also be a problem, what is a normal conversation to the student can feel a little like a shouting match to his classmates. Use these ideas to help your close-talker learn to back up and tone it down a little bit.

Indicators of Lack of Respect for Personal Space

- Stands very close to classmates when talking to them.

- Classmates back away from this student.

- Classmates need to scoot their chairs or desks away to have enough space.

- The student seems to take up her own desk space and part of her neighbor's too.

- Close talking may be accompanied by unwanted touching or overly loud volume.

Tips and Tricks for Managing a Student's Lack of Respect for Personal Space

- **Make personal space measurable by teaching students to hold their arms out in front of them when they are talking to each other.** If they can just touch each other's shoulders with their fingertips, then this is plenty of distance apart. (This is more space than many students actually need, but students are likely to creep in closer to each other as they chat, so this will help keep them apart as needed.)

- **Practice conversation distance.** Have students sit an appropriate distance apart from each other and chat quietly. Next, switch partners and have them stand on two X marks made with colored tape to chat again. Let them get used to the distance between them. Eventually, remove the tape. Watch to see if students maintain the distance they have gotten used to. After enough practice, the student with Asperger's (and any other close talkers) may get used to the correct amount of space their classmates are comfortable with.

- **Space boundaries at tables.** If students are seated at tables, divide the tables with colored tape so that students know what their space boundaries are.

- **Space boundaries at desks.** If students use desks, pull the leaning student's desk a few inches away from his neighbor's to give the neighbor more space.

- **First in line.** When students are walking in a line, have the student with Asperger's walk in the front of the line so he cannot walk too closely behind someone else.

- **Walking in line.** If the student walks in the middle or back of the line, ask him to periodically reach out a hand. If he can touch the classmate in front of him, he is too close and should slow down for a few steps.

- **Safety space on stairs.** When students are walking on stairs, remind them that there should be two steps between them and the person in front of them at all times, so students do not step on the backs of each other's feet.

- **Play "The Quiet Game."** Let students have uninterrupted time just to chat, on the condition that they do it quietly. If students start to get loud, turn off one bank of lights in the room to warn them about the volume. Listen to see whether the student with Asperger's quiets down along with the other students and gently remind him to adjust the volume as needed.

Inappropriate Physical Contact (Others and Self)

Physical contact that goes beyond a high five or fist bump, especially when it is not reciprocal, can be bothersome to classmates. Students with Asperger's may have trouble with impulse control, so when they see something they want to touch, grab, squeeze, or tackle, they may not be able to resist. Frustration with being touched can cause even kind classmates to retaliate if the situation is not kept under control. Educating the student who touches others, or even himself, inappropriately is necessary to keep the learning environment productive and safe for everyone.

Indicators of Inappropriate Physical Contact

- Student struggles with paying attention when another classmate is close by.

- Student sits close to others; seems to hover.

- Contact is made during inappropriate times.

- Classmates near the student seem constantly distracted.

- Classmates complain about being touched.

- Playground play seems unnecessarily rough, for example, constant tackling during flag football or soccer.

- Student is constantly bumping into others in the hallway or during floor-sitting times.

- Student has hands in his own clothing, especially in his underwear.

Tips and Tricks for Managing a Student's Inappropriate Physical Contact

- **Be clear about what kind of touching is acceptable in your classroom.** High fives, fist bumps, and handshakes are good touches. Other touching bothers classmates and is not acceptable in the classroom.

- **Acceptable and unacceptable touching.** Brainstorm a list of touching that is OK, if students do not seem to get the point. Then, post a list of the types of touching that are acceptable. When a student touches another, ask her if she sees that touch on the acceptable list. If it is not, she has broken a classroom rule. Because students with Asperger's are often very rigid about following rules, this approach may work for the student.

- **Often, we say, "Keep your hands to yourself,"** but students may not really understand what that means. Humorously demonstrate with a stuffed animal that has long arms, such as a sock monkey. Seat the sock monkey next to a student and show the sock monkey touching the student's arm. Next, show the monkey keeping its hands to itself. Let students tell you when the sock monkey is behaving well and when it is not. Let students tell the sock monkey how to keep its hands to itself and show what it means to do so.

- **Remove temptation.** Seat the student some distance away from others if she is having trouble keeping her hands or her work materials to herself. (You may need to explain that poking someone with a pencil is just as bad as touching the person.) Removing temptation may help her keep her mind on her work.

- **Give something tactile** such as a smooth stone or a squeezy ball to the student with Asperger's to encourage him to touch that instead of classmates.

- **A natural consequence.** If a student develops a habit of putting her hands in her pants, ask her to please wash her hands. Have a private conversation with the student about not putting her hands in her pants and explain that she will have to wash her hands every time this happens. From that point forward, have her wash her hands every time she does it (even if her hands are on the outside of her pants) in the hope of her getting tired of washing her hands and breaking the habit.

- **If self-touching is a problem because of easy access,** you may need to speak to parents about the clothing the student wears to school. Encourage them to send their child to school in long shorts or pants with fitted underwear. Explain that skirts and dresses without shorts or bloomers underneath (for girls) or loose athletic shorts (for boys) are not appropriate for their child at this time.

- **Good Hands and Good Feet worksheet (page 65).** Use this worksheet to help show students what kinds of touching are acceptable and what kinds are not.

Name: _____

Good Hands and Good Feet

Directions: Write the word **YES** in the blank box if the picture shows an **OK** way to touch a friend. Write the word **NO** in the blank box if the picture shows a way that it is **NOT OK** to touch a friend. Color the **YES** pictures.

Lack of Personal Care and Hygiene

While most teachers have to address hygiene with a student every now and then, it can be a particular problem with students with Asperger's because of sensory issues. The smell of soaps, the taste of mint toothpaste, the feel of a hairbrush or of washing in a tub—all of these things can be aggravating. Some students have a favorite piece of clothing that smells "just right" after a couple of days, and when it's washed, it does not smell "right" anymore. It is similar to young children who have "loveys" that they cannot bear to have washed. Parents may sometimes take the path of least resistance and let their child with Asperger's go without bathing or brushing their teeth in favor of keeping the peace, but classmates will soon pick up on the fact that the student is not clean. Here are some ideas for helping the resistant student understand why a regular hygiene routine is a good idea.

Indicators of Lack of Personal Care and Hygiene

- Seems poorly or inappropriately dressed for the weather; wears a heavy coat in warm weather or shorts in cold weather.

- Wears the same clothing over and over.

- Smells bad, seems dirty or smelly. Looks like he just rolls out of bed to come to school.

- Does not brush teeth on a regular basis.

- Classmates comment on the student's hygiene.

Tips and Tricks for Managing a Student's Lack of Personal Care and Hygiene

- **Healthy Hygiene Checklist (page 67).** Speak with parents to develop a game plan for getting the student to follow a hygiene routine. Use the Healthy Hygiene Checklist and give the student rewards for following it.

- **If scented products are the problem,** suggest that parents look into the many unscented soaps and shampoos now on the market.

- **Teach hygiene as a health and science unit.** If the student learns about some hygiene facts at school, it may make her more inclined to follow some of the routines. Have a school nurse or dentist visit as part of your unit to share hygiene facts. Some other possible science activities could be to test different soaps and toothpastes, test chewable tablets that highlight plaque in the mouth, try washing hands versus using antibacterial gel, and seeing which wipes clean the most dirt off of hands or desks.

- **Sensory hygiene issues.** If the student is working with a therapist of any sort, mention the sensory hygiene issues to the therapist and see if there is any related task that can be added to the student's routine that will help him overcome sensory aversions.

- **Explain some of the social consequences of having poor hygiene to the student.** As students get older, they may care more about how their peers perceive them and may be willing to take some steps to freshen their breath, wash their hair, etc., without putting up so much of a fight.

- **Insensitive to hot and cold temperatures.** Because students with Asperger's can be insensitive to hot and cold temperatures, come up with a fast rule—if the thermometer is below 50° F, no shorts are allowed because it is too cold. Similarly, if it is above 75° F, no coats are allowed because it is too warm.

Healthy Hygiene Checklist

Name: _____ **Date:** _____

TASKS →	I took a bath or shower.	I washed my face.	I brushed my teeth.	I brushed or combed my hair.	I put on clean clothes.
Days of the Week ↓					
Sunday					
Monday					
Tuesday					
Wednesday					
Thursday					
Friday					
Saturday					

Fear of Change, Need for Sameness in Daily Routine, and Rituals

While many students like the comfort of routines, students who tend toward Asperger's behaviors may want the same things to happen at the same times every day. Students with autism often have very rigid schedules, but those with Asperger's can sometimes learn to cope with changes. Often, you can reason with them that life does not unfold in the same way every day. This may help them adapt to change and maybe even learn to enjoy it.

In addition, as discussed, some students may develop certain rituals to keep themselves calm during times of stress and change. While it is great that they have developed their own ways to cope, the rituals may be elaborate, time-consuming, or strange. They may disturb others or may take so much time for the student to complete that they disrupt your regular classroom routine and prevent you from getting through your lesson plans. If this is the case, you need to develop strategies to help this student get past the rituals more quickly.

Indicators of a High Need for Sameness in Daily Routine

- Says things such as, "I did not get to do _____" at a change in the routine and then seems upset about it.

- Argues when something changes, as though you have done something wrong. May start sentences with, "But, you said…"

- Frequently asks what is coming next—this is how you know you haven't prepared a student enough.

- Is anxious about uncertainty in the daily schedule.

- Acts out or uses comfort speech or other self-soothing behavior at any change in schedule.

- Repeatedly does not complete work, to the point where you have to question the student and possibly do observations to find out what is happening.

Tips and Tricks for Managing a Student's High Need for Sameness in Daily Routine

- **Be prepared to explain ahead of time what the day's or week's schedule is.** It is not enough for these students just to tell them what comes next; you have to give them the big picture. This is somewhat true for all students, but intensely so for the student with Asperger's who fears change. Written, posted schedules provide a feeling of safety.

- **"Why are there changes?"** This student will want to know why changes are coming, so take time to explain your reasons for making changes as well. For example, if you are not able to spend your normal time on the playground, you will need to tell the student that it is because of grass mowing or because it rained, and it is too muddy. Knowing the "why" will usually reduce anxiety and prevent arguing.

- **Special activities and therapy services cause anxiety for many students with Asperger's because they are outside of the classroom.** They are a break in the routine, and they are different every day. Make a calendar with the special classes on it. Distribute it to students and parents and post a large copy in the classroom to help students remember when special classes or activities happen each day so that they can prepare for them. Verbally remind students of the special classes they have each day by going over the posted calendar as part of your morning meeting.

- **If a student frequently comes in late,** talk with parents about how much anxiety this causes, especially if specials happen in the morning or if the student misses announcements about other changes in the routine.

- **What's Happening This Week? worksheet (page 71).** This worksheet can help students who are anxious about the week's events by preparing them for extra changes in the routine. You can use it as a weekly calendar for all students and also write in any changes that are coming up so that they will not be surprised.

- **Be careful not to plan more than you can accomplish.** Assuming you can get more done than you actually have time for can cause you to rush through your day or can cause you not to check off all of the items on your posted calendar. This stresses out students with Asperger's because they like to see everything checked off. Always under-plan your day slightly so that students see that everything on the list gets checked off as often as possible. If you are left with extra time, then students will know that time is always for reading, math fact practice, etc.

- **As you write on the board or schedule your daily lesson plans, be specific but also open-ended.** This sounds like a tall order, but it really is simple. You want the lessons you carry out to be recognizable as what you said you were going to do, but not so rigid that the student knows that you had to make a change. Leave yourself some wiggle room so that you still feel free to make a change if you need to. For example, if you want to work on the 12, 13, and 14 fact families in your math period, it is more than sufficient to say you are going to work on fact families in math, without saying which ones. That way, if you get through 12 and 13 but not 14, no one but you will know you are behind.

- **Keeping the peace.** When you have to make a change in a routine that truly cannot be helped, it is OK to say that it was someone else's decision (who is not available to argue with the student with Asperger's) in order to keep the peace. For example, if you have to eat lunch in the classroom instead of the lunchroom because the lunchroom is being painted that day, explain that your principal said that no one is allowed to go into the lunchroom that day, and you have to follow the rules. This student, who may love rules, can usually understand that everyone has to follow rules, even the teacher.

- **Some students have elaborate rituals that take up large chunks of class time or other valuable time.** For example, you may have a student who takes a long time to start her work because there she has too many preparation rituals such as taking all of the pencils out of her pencil box and repacking it every time she needs to use a pencil. Before you deal with the rituals, do some observations so that you have plenty of information about what they are and when they occur.

- **Encourage shorter "routine times."** If you have a student who has a long or exceptionally rigid routine that must happen before beginning work or eating lunch, chip away at the time it takes for the student to get started. Your first step to negotiating a shorter routine may be breaking it down into smaller pieces so that you can start convincing the student to eliminate steps. For example, if she needs to sharpen every pencil every morning, ask that she only keep three pencils in her desk.

- **Ask for parental help.** If the student is very resistant to shortening her routine to the point where it really upsets her day, ask her parents to start part of the routine at home or to bring her to school earlier to start the routine so that she can finish it on time. For example, if her routine involves washing her desk inside and out, have her clean it while other students are packing up in the afternoon instead of in the morning. If she really must sharpen every pencil, have her sharpen them at home before she leaves for school.

- **Ask the student to make his own routine checklist** if moving parts of the routine to different times or to home seem to agitate him. Checking off tasks will give him more control over making sure they still get completed, even if they are not completed at school as he is used to doing.

- **Some students become very attached to objects from home when they become part of a ritual.** If your student brings an object that is large or electronic, it will be a big distraction for others. Work with parents to replace it with something else or find a way to leave it at home. For example, if the student brings in a noisy electronic calculator, allow it to come to class, but insist that the batteries be removed.

- **Depending on the student's age, try reasoning with her.** She may rationally know that she does not need the sameness, or the ritual, or even the object, but insists on doing it anyway. If you can sit with her and explain why she needs to be OK with going to the gym when it rains, or why she needs to stop insisting on going to the bathroom four times before she is ready to work, or why she cannot bring her weather radio to class anymore, she may be able to understand your reasoning and work with you.

- **Finally, be flexible.** Rituals can be an important coping mechanism. Stopping a ritual can make a student feel worried and uncertain, so proceed with patience and only when it is really necessary. If the ritual is not hurting anyone or disrupting the classroom, it may be better to wait and see if it subsides on its own.

What's Happening This Week?

Name: _____ **Date:** _____

Monday	Tuesday	Wednesday	Thursday	Friday
Lunchtime: Special: Changes:	Lunchtime: Special: Changes:	Lunchtime: Special: Changes:	Lunchtime: Special: Changes:	Lunchtime: Special: Changes:

KE-804111 © Carson-Dellosa

Tips for Teaching Kids with Asperger's

Problems with Nonverbal Communication

Think about how many facial expressions you use with students each day, such as silly faces, stern looks, and raised eyebrows. Imagine if you had a student who could see you but could not understand your facial expressions. A student who can read your expressions and body language is ahead of the game, while a student who cannot misses out on a great deal of the tone behind what you are saying.

Missing out on nonverbal communication also prevents the student from being able to joke with friends, and that becomes very important starting in early elementary school. "Sense of humor" is one of the most desirable traits in friends and partners. People who find each other funny are able to bond easily. Students who are stiff or formal or who do not understand why everyone else is laughing have a harder time finding and keeping friends. The kid who "doesn't get it" is usually not the kid that everyone else wants to be friends with.

In addition, when students do not react to nonverbal cues and body language, they are not likely to understand how to communicate in that way either. So, if someone tells a sad story, this student may lack a sympathetic expression. Classmates often mistake this as a sign that this student is cold and unfeeling. The opposite may be true, but the student is not very good at showing emotions or even understanding what emotions to show. Classmates can feel very justified in disliking a student with Asperger's because they do not seem kind or caring, but the student may simply not know how to show empathy. This behavior, for students with Asperger's, may have to be learned.

Although it is not part of the curriculum, you may find yourself doing a little emotional coaching to keep the peace in your classroom. Because communication in group work is such an important part of students' education, you have to make sure groups can function well. And, of course, you want your students to get along and be kind to each other. You are sure to have questions from some parents about whether their children are making friends. If your student with Asperger's seems at a loss for this type of communication, here are some ways to help.

Indicators of Problems with Nonverbal Communication

- Does not seem to need to look at people when they are talking and is often unable to pick up on facial expressions and body language.

- Does not always respond to or pick up on body language, such as when another student turns around and stomps off in anger.

- Does not respond with sympathy when a student is sad or gets hurt.

- Does not respond with facial expressions.

- Facial expressions do not match her words.

- Seems very literal.

- Does not seem to "get" jokes.

- May be a beat behind on laughing at funny things in the classroom.

- Talks like a little adult; does not act silly with friends.

- When they do act silly, it is not age-appropriate—seems extremely juvenile for their age.

- May not use hand gestures when they talk to emphasize what is being said.

- May have an odd tone of voice.

Tips and Tricks for Dealing with Problems with Nonverbal Communication

- **Think about your facial expressions.** When you talk to this student, think about your facial expressions and make sure you are backing them up with your language so there is no miscommunication.

- **Match your words with your facial expressions.** Try to build a comfortable relationship with that student and explain that he should ask you about any kind of communication with classmates that he does not understand.

- **Role-play using body language and facial expressions.** If the student has a therapist or social skills teacher, ask if there are some ways to role-play different types of body language and facial expressions. There is no way to prepare the student for every new facial expression, but she can learn to recognize common signals such as stomping feet and folded arms.

- **Stock your classroom with books about feelings and emotions,** such as *How Are You Peeling?* by Saxton Freymann and Joost Elffers (Scholastic Paperbacks, 2004), which shows facial expressions and talks about emotions in a clever, unusual way.

- **Picture book characters.** Remind students to look at facial expressions of picture book characters to help them understand what characters are feeling and to reinforce experience with facial expressions.

- **Body Language Charades worksheet (page 75).** Role-play body language as a class. Cut apart the Body Language Charades cards and put the slips of paper in a hat. Let each student draw a slip and act out the words listed on the paper using only facial expressions and body language. Have students raise their hands to be called on to guess the emotion or feeling they are trying to show. The student who guesses correctly can draw the next paper. Make sure the student with Asperger's gets to perform at least once and has several chances to guess. This is a great activity to fill extra time at the end of your day.

- **I Look Happy! I Look Sad! worksheet (page 76).** This is just as hard to explain as it is to teach, but visuals go a long way toward training a student who has a difficult time recognizing facial cues and body language. Use the I Look Happy! I Look Sad! worksheet to help students practice recognizing facial cues. They can use it in two ways. Let students use it as a conventional worksheet. Sit with the student who is having a hard time and let her tell you what she thinks each expression means. Then, copy the worksheet for half of the class and write the expressions on the cards. Pair students with partners. Let students take turns looking at each card and, without showing it to her partner, make the face to see if her partner can guess what expression she is making. (Also use this worksheet to teach inference during a reading comprehension lesson.)

- **Have a day for students to dress like their favorite characters.** Ask students to remain "in character" for a period of time. They should walk, talk, and act like the characters as much as possible, using appropriate facial expressions, voices, and body language that the characters would use.

- **Try practicing and performing a class play.** You may discover that your student with Asperger's has great acting talent, because he may already be mimicking others' actions and facial expressions much of the time to fit in with classmates. A part in a play will give the student even more practice and allow him to showcase his talent.

- **Use the Body Language worksheet (page 77)** for a more abstract exercise in understanding how people communicate nonverbally, or simply as part of a writing lesson. Let each student look at the four different scenes on the page. Have each student choose one scenario and write or dictate a paragraph that tells what emotion the person in the picture is feeling. Ask the student why he thinks the person feels that way, giving details to back up his opinion. Depending on the age of your students, you may choose to have them do the writing themselves or dictate their answers to your assistant or a volunteer, to write about one scenario or to work on more than one. Also, you can use this as an assessment for how well your student with Asperger's is able to read nonverbal cues or as a teaching tool to show the student how to look for cues.

Body Language Charades

Teacher Directions: Each box contains a feeling or emotion word. Copy and cut apart the boxes. Put them in a hat. Let a student draw a slip and silently act out the emotion or feeling. Have classmates try to guess what the student is acting out. Call on classmates until someone guesses correctly. The guesser may draw the next slip of paper. Continue until everyone has a turn to act.

cold	hot	happy	sad
mad	scared	hungry	sleepy
angry	laughing	confused	jolly
tickled	itchy	annoyed	worried
weak	strong	upset	surprised
curious	bored	shy	frustrated

I Look Happy! I Look Sad!

Directions: What emotion do you think each person is feeling? Write the name for that emotion on the line.

 Tips for Teaching Kids with Asperger's

Body Language

Directions: Share what you think is happening in each picture.

Inflexibility or Rigid Thinking

Students with Asperger's may see things in black and white. At times, they are unable to see others' points of view. In academics, sometimes they can only see one right answer or one way to solve a problem. This is not unusual in many young students, but a student with Asperger's can be especially eager to vigorously defend her point of view. If you are discussing more than one way to do something in class, inflexibility becomes a problem in the classroom. Inflexibility and rigid thinking cause problems during group work. The student with Asperger's may sometimes feel that he must be the boss because doing things anyone else's way will not yield good results. Here are some suggestions for helping the student loosen up a little and look at things from others' point of view once in a while.

Indicators of Inflexibility or Rigid Thinking

- Shows frustration and aggravation, or even disbelief, that there is more than one right answer, more than one right way to do things, or more than one way to get places.

- Shows frustration with things that have a lot of exceptions such as spelling patterns, geometry, computation, and even scheduling.

- Tries to "argue down" students and teachers with different points of view.

- Prefers fact-based learning.

- Does not accept different interpretations for fiction.

- Struggles with writing, reading fiction, poetry, estimation, or any academic area where the point is not to just "find the answer."

- May think those who disagree with him are just wrong.

- Constantly assumes leadership positions in group work and partner work.

Tips and Tricks for Dealing with Inflexibility or Rigid Thinking

- **More than one way.** When learning is not just fact-based, explain ahead of time that there is more than one answer or more than one way to arrive at the answer. Don't spring it on the student who is likely to be frustrated, unless you really have to as part of the lesson.

- **Be patient.** You may have to offer more explanation than usual as to why different answers are not wrong. Be patient and give a lot of examples.

- **Frustration with a lack of a definite answer can easily lead to an upset student.** Be prepared for more emotion than usual and ask for parents' assistance if you sense the student is getting frustrated with particular lessons and you think the parents can comfort the student.

- **A new way of doing things.** If a student gets frustrated with gray areas, in some ways it is not much different from dealing with a typical student who gets frustrated with not having the "right" answer. Often, it is a matter of sitting down with the student and walking her through a new way of doing things. Remember, it is not that she cannot understand, but she just may not be able to understand right at that moment and needs time to get used to the new idea of not knowing an exact number or word as the answer.

- **Remember to use concrete examples as often as possible.** For example, when you are teaching fact families, and a student does not understand how the numerals can move around in equations but still give the same answers, use counters, apples, cars, or anything else that the student likes to demonstrate how fact families actually work.

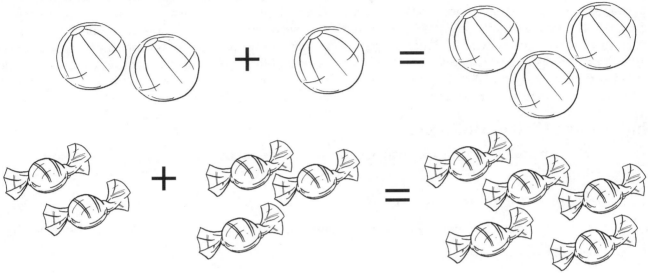

- **Not everyone thinks the same way.** For more abstract concepts, such as opinions, sometimes you just have to say, "Not everyone thinks the same way," and encourage the student to move on. This is a new concept to many elementary school students, not just for students with Asperger's.

- **Difficult group dynamics.** Carefully watch the groups that this student is part of, as you may have to deal with difficult group dynamics more often. Consider assigning well-defined roles to all group members so that no one student tries to be the boss of all of the others.

Talking to Themselves

Most people talk to themselves. Very young children do it quite naturally as they pretend, and it serves the important purpose of helping them solve conflicts and learn to tackle different social situations. It is a healthy part of having an active imagination. As children grow up, they still pretend but learn over time that talking to themselves is something most people do silently. Gradually, this tendency fades in most people. However, even adults with Asperger's may often talk aloud to themselves when other people are around and even talk back to TV shows and movies. Internal speech can be difficult to master, and talking out loud about every little thing can disrupt classmates. Note, too, that this kind of talking back is different from random speech, comfort speech, and echolalia. The student is often not repeating things or comforting herself. This speech is conversational. Here are some ideas for helping the student internalize the dialog.

Indicators of Talking to Themselves

- Talks to herself and waits for imaginary answers, unheard by others. (She is pretending to have a conversation.)

- May also give the answers in a conversation.

- Discusses things about her day, such as what she is doing next, in a way you would do in your own head.

- Asks and answers her own questions.

- Talks back to videos shown in class.

- May talk during live performances.

- May deny talking if you ask her to stop, because she assumes you mean to stop talking to another person.

Tips and Tricks for Dealing with Talking to Themselves

- **Realize that these students process things out loud instead of internally.** This can help them to relieve stress, process information, etc. This can be a large part of why students talk a lot in class anyway—they are still making the transition to learning to process things in their head. This understanding may help you be more patient while you wait to see progress.

- **Explain to classmates that one student may need to talk out loud sometimes.** Eventually, they may come to accept and then ignore it.

- **Allow times during class for students to take two minutes to explain a concept to a neighbor.** This technique relieves the student's need to process things out loud, and it helps students work on team problem solving.

- **Encourage other means of communication.** Ask the student to write his thoughts in a journal, on a computer, etc. This need may translate into better writing skills as it reduces the need for talking aloud.

- **Pair students with partners** as often as possible to work on in-class projects.

- **For younger students, assign oral reading.** This contributes to fluency as well.

- **Seating arrangements.** Seat the student who is very chatty in a remote part of the classroom so that he is less likely to disturb others.

- **Allow the student to take little breaks to chat with herself.** For example, send the student to the listening area or reading corner by herself to give her some alone time to chat. Do it subtly, because other students may get resentful when they cannot take frequent breaks too.

- **Any sanctioned chance to talk is a welcome break for this student.** Call the student up to the board to explain something, along with other students, so that he gets a chance to talk. Also, call on several different students to add to each other's answers. This gives more students a chance to contribute and to practice speaking to the class, and it gives the student with Asperger's a chance to speak.

- **Make a "chat phone"** by gluing together two curved pieces of PVC pipe. Give the phone to the student who needs to talk to herself. The phone will allow her to hear herself quite well; she will have to whisper to hear herself without hurting her ears. This can help you keep the volume down even when she talks to herself.

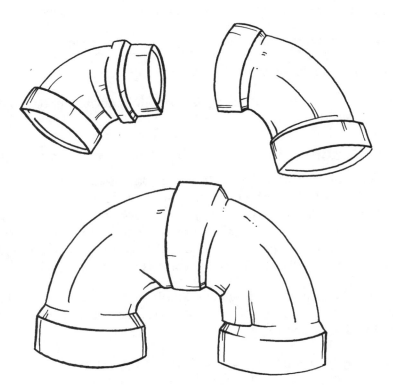

Inability to Start or Join a Conversation

Conversations, particularly social ones that are not part of classroom learning, can be like minefields for students with Asperger's. Students with Asperger's may see everyone else playing this fun "game" of chatting and having a good time, but they have no idea how to play, what the rules are, or even how to get in the game. Many students with Asperger's understand some of the mechanics of gathering in a group and saying things to each other that are by turns funny and serious, but that may be as close as they come to really joining in unless they are given some ground rules for how to play the game.

Again, this may not seem like actual academic instruction, but it does benefit the atmosphere of your classroom if all students are able to participate fully. Class discussion is weighted as part of students' grades—more so as they get older. So, preparing your students to talk to each other as part of their grades will also help them learn the life skill of talking to each other.

Indicators of an Inability to Start or Join a Conversation

- Stands in a group of friends and looks eager or impatient to talk, but never does.

- Starts or joins conversations in a bizarre way, with a strange or irrelevant question or comment.

- Gets frustrated to the point of interrupting, anger, or tears when talking with friends.

- Raises hand in class, but frequently has nothing to say when called on.

- Seems lost during group discussions of any kind.

- Classmates seem to talk right over this student or briefly acknowledge what he says and then move on without really including him.

Tips and Tricks for Dealing with an Inability to Start or Join a Conversation

- **First, remember that making conversation is a sophisticated skill.** If you have students who do not spend a lot of time having conversations at home, it is a skill everyone will have a hard time with, not just your students with Asperger's. So, give step-by-step instructions for starting a conversation. Tell students to make eye contact, check that there is enough personal space, smile and look friendly, try not to cross their arms, say something simple such as, "Hi," ask a question, listen for a response, and say something about the response. Then, the conversation should pick up from there.

- **Role-play situations** such as meeting new people of different ages or asking a question to start a conversation. Even simple lessons about smiling at someone or making eye contact can help students feel more comfortable talking to people.

- **Teach some generic conversation starters.** Give some examples. For example, talk about sitting across from a friend at the lunch table. Ask, "How can you start a conversation with your friend?" Students might suggest asking what they have for lunch today or asking what their favorite TV show is, what music they like to listen to, or what sports they play. Challenge students to have at least one conversation with a friend at lunch that day and then get them to report back who they talked to and what they talked about.

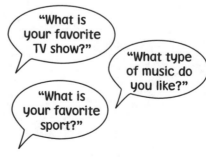

- **Teach students not to ask questions with yes or no answers.** These answers do not make conversations go further. Instead, help students come up with open-ended alternatives. For example, instead of asking, "Did you watch TV last night," ask, "What TV show did you watch last night?"

- **Tape a few conversations and help the student listen for natural pauses.** Stop the tape when she hears a pause and ask, "OK, what could you say there?"

- **Learning to think and listen.** Explain that when you are thinking about what you want to say, it is easy to forget about listening to what others are saying. You have to multitask. If you do not, then what you want to say may no longer be relevant when the break in the conversation comes.

- **Disconnected conversations.** Students with Asperger's may hear conversations and think of a comment that is not connected in an obvious way. You may need to teach them to say something such as, "What you said made me think of …" In other words, show them how to verbally build a bridge from the conversation to what they want to add to the conversation.

- **Eat with students.** Because lunchtime is a prime social time for many students, if you choose to eat lunch elsewhere, enlist volunteer "spies" to eat lunch with your students. Ask for parent volunteers to sit with students and report back to you about what they are talking about and what slang they are using. Plus, students will use their conversation skills and see adults model theirs.

- **Play a conversation game with students.** During desk-work time, invite one student at a time to come up to your desk and talk to you. The trick is that the student must initiate the conversation by asking you a question about yourself. Or, turn this into more of a lesson by discussing a student's favorite book or the topic chosen for a school project. You can then keep the conversation going. Try to spend five minutes chatting with each student who comes to your desk. Mark off each student so you can keep track of who has had a turn. If possible, give the student with Asperger's a few extra chances to chat.

- **Write a conversation.** After you read a book, have students write about a conversation that two characters from the book might have. Let each student choose her own two favorite characters and write the conversation or let students work in pairs to do it. Have students read their conversations back to the class.

Tangential Conversations

Once a student with Asperger's is included in a conversation, his worries usually are not over. Unless he gets lucky and the topic is one he loves to discuss (which has its own issues), he still has to navigate staying on topic. This can be tricky, because his tendency might be to zoom in on an offhand comment that interests him much more than the main topic at hand. For example, in a conversation about a recent science fiction movie that had music that sounded like another science fiction movie, it might be very hard for the student with Asperger's not to take off on a tangent about all of the famous movie figures he owns. This leap off into another direction can frustrate classmates who are anxious to continue talking about the movie they all just saw—not their friend's toys. Following are some ideas for helping the student keep track of the main idea of the conversation.

Indicators of Tangential Conversations

- Cannot seem to follow the thread of a conversation.

- Tries to draw the conversation around to his own interests, even if they are not directly related.

- Talks about the same few topics repeatedly.

- Always references her reading and writing assignments back to the same few topics.

- Classmates say, for example, "I do not want to talk to Lynn. She always wants to talk about tornadoes."

Tips and Tricks for Tangential Conversations

- **Discourage long soliloquies.** Adults especially are willing to tolerate long soliloquies about topics that children are very interested in. Well-meaning adults who think this behavior is cute encourage this "little professor" behavior. It can be endearing to hear a three-year-old speak enthusiastically about roller coasters, but the result is that students often enter school having had this behavior indulged to the point where the student believes that everyone is truly interested in hearing long lists of facts about her favorite topics. This can be a hard habit to break, so proceed gently.

- **Gently redirect the student when the conversation starts to stray.** Say, for example, "Thank you, Mara, for telling us about animals, but we need to talk about how the leaves are changing on the trees now. Do you have anything to say about that?" Give her time to get back on track and start speaking again about the topic you brought up.

- **Cutting off conversations.** When you are teaching, do not be afraid to cut the student off in the interest of time and summarize the parts of her answer that are on topic. Although this may feel rude, it gives her an example of what the length of time of an answer should be. And, you are modeling that answering a teacher's question is different from having a conversation with friends.

- **Importance of listening.** Conversely, emphasize the importance of hearing friends out during conversations. Read more about this in the Difficulty with Turn-Taking section found on page 87.

- **Make a list with the student of his favorite topics.** The student may not realize how many times he goes to the same topic until you gently point it out to him. This will help him steer clear of the same old favorites and may help him stay on topic during class discussion.

- **Monitor yourself** and make sure you are not leading the way in getting off topic as you teach—it is easy to do!

- **Students may be so compelled to talk about their favorite topics** that they will use any means to get there. For example, they will come to your desk and say, "I need to ask you something," and then launch into a long story about the topic you are trying to steer them away from. First, make sure there is no important question tucked into the story and then gently get them back on track.

- **Write about favorite topics.** If the need to talk about the topic is so strong that the student has trouble resisting it, encourage her to write about it at writing time or draw about it during art.

- **Keep count.** Let students write tally marks or use craft sticks to keep track of how many times they talk about their favorite topics. This is not meant to be punitive; rather, it helps students who are old enough to try to control this behavior to be more aware of how many times they are talking about their favorite topics during school each day.

- **Perseveration can also be a gift.** Remember, while dealing with this issue of talking about a favorite topic takes patience, this type of perseveration can also be a gift. If you have a student who really wants to explore the topic further, let her run with it until she is an absolute expert. Give the student an outlet in the way of a class project by having her write a book, create a poster, conduct a science experiment, or complete a social studies project. Who knows, that tornado obsession today could turn into a career in weather forecasting tomorrow!

- **Use the My Favorite Topic worksheet (page 86)** to give the student a chance to expound on his favorite topic. Let him answer questions, draw pictures, and even do some research. Allow students to present their favorite topics to the class to give everyone in the class a chance to shine.

Name: _____

My Favorite Topic

Directions: You are going to tell the entire class about your favorite topic. It can be any topic you choose: a sport, a game, an animal, a place you like to visit, something in nature, a person, or anything at all. Use this page to help you learn more about it.

Topic I chose: _____

Why I chose it: _____
_____
_____

Picture of my topic:

Research I did (Look up two sources about your topic.): _____
_____
_____

Five cool things I know about my topic: 1. _____
2. _____ 3. _____
4. _____ 5. _____

One other thing I want you to remember: _____
_____
_____

My Favorite Topic

Directions: You are going to tell the entire class about your favorite topic. It can be any topic you choose: a sport, a game, an animal, a place you like to visit, something in nature, a person, or anything at all. Use this page to help you learn more about it.

Topic I chose: _____

Why I chose it: _____

_____

_____

Picture of my topic:

Research I did (Look up two sources about your topic.): _____

_____

_____

Five cool things I know about my topic: 1. _____

2. _____ 3. _____

4. _____ 5. _____

One other thing I want you to remember: _____

_____

_____

_____

Difficulty with Turn Taking

Students often compete for more talking time in the classroom, and the competition can be fierce. Curbing the impulse to shout over others can be a teacher's constant battle with a particularly noisy class. With pairs and small groups, it can be hard to train students to listen carefully and absorb what others are saying, as well as to wait for conversation partners to finish speaking before taking a turn to talk. Many students have trouble treating what others say as something they should actually hear, rather than time during which they should gather their thoughts until the next time they get a chance to speak. Learning to take turns means learning patience and listening skills, and all of these will benefit students in the classroom.

Indicators of Difficulty with Turn Taking

- Starts taking a breath to speak before someone else is finished speaking.

- Raises hand in class before you finish speaking.

- Does not have an answer when called on—is raising hand just to make sure to get the turn.

- Frequently talks over others or interrupts.

- Asks a question and does not wait for the answer or gives the answer himself.

Tips and Tricks for Difficulty with Turn Taking

- **Encourage families to have dinner together.** Because of modern parenting schedules, students may spend little time listening to adults talking to each other. Encourage families to have dinner together when possible so that students have opportunities to listen to adult conversations, where they will hopefully hear turn-taking, quiet voices, and examples of good listening.

- **Explain the term "wait time."** Younger students may not be able to do this, but older students may be able to learn to silently count to three after someone else finishes talking before they start talking so that they do not interrupt or cut others off.

- **Enforce talking only while raising hands.** Students are often tempted to shout out answers in class, and making them raise their hands reinforces wait time so that it may be present during class discussions as well.

- **Structure your classroom so that listening is valued as much as talking.** Instead of lecturing the whole time, ask questions and then give students plenty of time to respond. Value what they have to say as much as you expect them to value what you have to say. Be sure to ask their opinions often to give them chances to speak.

- **Pair students with partners to practice conversations in the classroom,** so that each only has one other person to compete with while talking. Remind students that listening is as important as talking and then have them summarize what their conversation partners said to check how well they listened.

- **Make eye contact.** As students talk to each other, remind them how important it is to look at each other. This may be hard for students with Asperger's to do, because they do not like to make eye contact. In these cases, offer a student other cues to let you know she is listening and waiting for her turn, such as saying, "I am still listening," or using body language such as nodding her head or giving a thumbs up.

- **Videotape Observations worksheet (page 89).** Videotape students having conversations, either in pairs or during group work. Let them practice talking to a few different classmates and then match up new pairs to talk to each other. As you watch each video, point out things such as how often they spoke, whether they interrupted each other or took turns, what their body language was like, how long they wanted to talk to each other, and whether the pair or group worked well together. This exercise would work well for showing students any number of interesting things about their conversation habits. Use the Videotape Observations worksheet to make observations about each pair of students so you can discuss conversations specifically with them later. If you do not want to videotape a pair or group, you or an adult volunteer can observe the group and make notes from the observations on the worksheet.

- **Nothing teaches turn taking like playing games.** This can be a lot of work and take a lot of patience on your part, but playing card games and board games will eventually teach students that they have to wait for their turns in order for games to go well. If possible, invite parents into your classroom and have each parent monitor a different group so that someone is there to make sure the rules are followed, everyone gets their turn, and the competitiveness does not get out of hand (particularly with students with Asperger's).

- **Purchase a few plastic toy microphones from a dollar store.** Assign groups and spread out in a big area, such as the gym, and give each group one microphone. Explain that only the student who has the microphone can do any talking, and let students talk to each other about anything they want. Blow a whistle and let the students talk. When you blow the whistle again, have students hand off their microphones. Continue until everyone gets a turn.

- **If students can read well enough, assign them parts in short, in-class plays.** Give each part to a different student, have them rehearse reading their parts in a circle, and then let each group read their play aloud. Emphasize how each person must wait until the person before is completely finished until the next person speaks. Change names as needed to suit the genders in your class.

Name: _____

Videotape Observations

Directions: Make observations about each pair's or group's conversation, so later you can talk about specific aspects of it.

Date: _____

Pair or Group Members: _____

Did all of the pairs or group members talk to each other? How much? _____

_____

_____

How did the pairs or group members work together? _____

_____

_____

_____

_____

Other observations: _____

_____

_____

_____

_____

Here are some suggestions for other observations you can share and questions you can ask the group:
- Count seconds between responses to check for appropriate wait time.
- What was the topic? Did the group stay on topic?
- List nonverbal cues used by different students.
- Did conversation between all students seem natural?
- On a scale of 1–5, with 5 as the highest, how would you rate the group's performance?
- Ask group members what they would do differently next time.

Asking Pertinent Questions and Giving Appropriate Answers

Asking questions is part of taking the initiative in a conversation. It is important to teach this skill. Students need to ask good questions to get the information they need. Giving students with Asperger's the skill of asking questions helps them take a break from talking for long stretches. Plus, if students ask questions, others are more likely to be interested in talking with them for a longer period of time, thus giving them practice with all of the other important conversation skills.

To ask questions, students must be able to figure out if the questions in their heads are actually pertinent to what is going on in the conversation at the time. For example, it is not uncommon for a student with Asperger's to ask a question relevant to the conversation ten minutes before, or that is only vaguely related to what is happening now, or that is only related in a way that the student understands.

Equally important is that a student understands how to answer a question. Nothing is more frustrating to a teacher than asking for an answer to a math fact, being delighted to see a student raise her hand, only to have her ask, "May I get a tissue?" Knowing how to answer a question has obvious academic applications for all students. Understanding how to ask pertinent questions and give relevant answers will help students with all kinds of testing and with class participation grades.

Indicators of Difficulty with Asking Pertinent Questions and Waiting for Answers

- Rarely asks questions in class, even when the student does not understand the work.

- Asks questions that are unrelated to what is going on in a conversation or discussion.

- Does little to help others engage with him in conversations.

- Gives answers that do not relate to the question asked.

- Rapidly fires questions at you without waiting for answers.

- Tunes you out before you finish giving answers.

- Raises a hand to give an answer but then has nothing to say.

Tips and Tricks for Difficulty with Asking Pertinent Questions and Waiting for Answers

- **Classroom interviews.** At the beginning of the year, have students write five questions they would like to ask a new friend. Suggest that students use the five Ws here (who, what, where, when, and why). Pair them to interview each other.

- **Use the Ask the Right Questions worksheet (page 92).** Sometimes, breaking into a conversation is as simple as showing interest by asking the right question. A student with Asperger's may have no idea how to do this. Use the Ask the Right Questions worksheet to show how this is done. For further practice, let students write other questions they could ask for each conversation on separate sheets of paper.

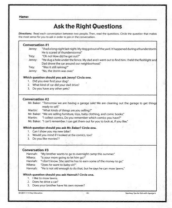

- **Ask Five Good Questions worksheet (page 94).** Read a paragraph right before it is time to do something that students look forward to, such as going outside to the playground. Tell them they will get their rewards right after they think of five good questions to ask about the paragraph. Using the Ask Five Good Questions worksheet can help guide students into thinking up their own questions.

- **KWL Chart (page 95).** Create class questions about a reading homework assignment the day before students tackle the reading. Do a KWL chart and model the "Want to Know" part for the class. After reviewing the reading homework the next day, revisit the chart and ask students if they learned anything they wanted to know. The KWL chart can help the students organize and visually see what they have learned.

- **Test questions.** If you have tests coming up, work hard on the practice test comprehension sections. These are full of examples of good questions and different ways to ask and answer them.

- **Giant punctuation marks.** Cut out a large circle (a period), a large exclamation point, and a large question mark from poster board. Give the three pieces of punctuation to three students. Let one student read a sentence that is either a statement, question, or exclamation. See if the three students know which punctuation to raise each time. Give this group a few more turns and then change to a new reader and new punctuation holders. Continue until everyone has had a turn.

- **Give Some Good Answers worksheet (page 93).** Knowing how to give relevant answers is as important as asking good questions. It is disappointing to have someone engaged in a conversation, get them to ask you a question, and answer them, only to have them give you a strange look and say, "Uh, okay…." Use the Give Some Good Answers worksheet which is similar to the Ask the Right Questions worksheet (page 92) to help guide students into giving relevant answers.

Ask the Right Questions

Directions: Read each conversation between two people. Then, read the questions. Circle the question that makes the most sense for you to ask to join in the conversation.

Conversation #1

Jenny: "I had a long night last night. My dog got out of the yard. It happened during a thunderstorm. He is scared of thunderstorms!"

Trey: "Oh no! How did he get out?"

Jenny: "He dug a hole under the fence. My dad and I went out to find him. I held the flashlight, and Dad drove the car around our neighborhood."

Trey: "Was it still raining?"

Jenny: "No, the storm was over."

Which question should you ask Jenny? Circle one.

1. Did you ever find your dog?
2. What kind of car did your dad drive?
3. Do you have any other pets?

Conversation #2

Mr. Baker: "Tomorrow we are having a garage sale! We are cleaning out the garage to get things ready to sell."

Martin: "What kinds of things are you selling?"

Mr. Baker: "We are selling furniture, toys, baby clothing, and comic books."

Martin: "I collect comics. Do you remember which comics you have?"

Mr. Baker: "I can't remember. I can get them out for you to look at if you like."

Which question should you ask Mr. Baker? Circle one.

1. Can I show you my new bike?
2. Would you mind if I looked at the comic, too?
3. Do you like movies?

Conversation #3

Hannah: "My brother wants to go to overnight camp this summer."

Nikera: "Is your mom going to let him go?"

Hannah: "I don't know. She said he has to earn some of the money to go."

Nikera: "Does he want to babysit?"

Hannah: "He is not old enough to do that, but he says he can mow lawns."

Which question should you ask Hannah? Circle one.

1. Do you like to mow lawns?
2. Does your brother drive a car?
3. Does your brother have his own mower?

Give Some Good Answers

Directions: Read each conversation. As you read, pretend you are talking to a friend. Then, read the answers to the questions. Circle the answer that makes the most sense.

Conversation #1

You: "I like tornadoes a lot. I am learning a lot about them."

Janal: "Really? Why do you like them?"

You: "I think they are pretty interesting, even though they are dangerous. They can pop up so fast and go away just as quickly."

Janal: "Is that what makes them so dangerous?"

Which answer makes the most sense? Circle one.

1. I have never been in a tornado. I would love to see one.
2. That's one thing. The other is that their wind speeds can reach almost 200 miles an hour.
3. Tornado Alley is located in the central plains of the United States.

Conversation #2

Jordan: "Can you come over to my house tomorrow?"

You: "I will have to ask my mom if it is OK. "

Jordan: "Here is my phone number. Get your mom to call us tonight."

You: "OK. I will ask her to."

Jordan: "What kinds of stuff do you like to play?"

Which answer makes the most sense? Circle one.

1. I have three dogs at home.
2. My sister likes to play with dolls a lot.
3. I like video games, I like to play basketball, and I like to do art too.

Conversation #3

You: "My favorite books are the ones about Geronimo Stilton."

Seth: "What are they about?"

You: "Geronimo is a mouse that edits a newspaper and goes on adventures."

Seth: "Are they funny books?"

Which answer makes the most sense? Circle one.

1. Yes, because Geronimo is kind of afraid of everything.
2. Geronimo gets into a lot of trouble.
3. He goes to find mummies in Egypt and searches for buried treasure.

Ask Five Good Questions

Directions: Listen to the paragraph that your teacher will read.
Think of five good questions to ask about the paragraph and write them down.

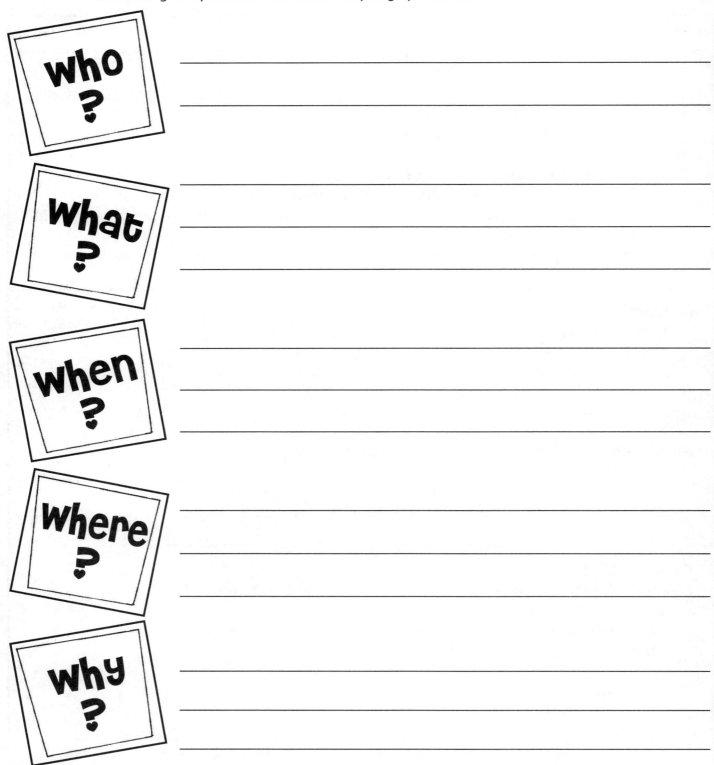

 **KWL** Chart

Topic: _____

I **K**now	
I **W**ant to know	
I **L**earned	

Immaturity

Students with Asperger's often are very book smart, but they may not seem to fit in with peers. In particular, they may not get "in" jokes and nuances of others' behavior and comments, especially when sarcasm is involved. This is not so much of a problem with very young students, who are not very subtle, but it becomes an increasing problem with upper elementary students. Asperger's students may be teased from an early age and often do not even realize if they are the targets of jokes. When they do realize it, they may not know what's funny. Sometimes, solving this problem in your classroom is more of a matter of educating classmates about kindness than it is educating the student about pop culture or slang. Here are some ways to build a kinder classroom while bringing the student with Asperger's up to speed.

Indicators of Immaturity

- May have an easier time socializing with younger students.

- Does not laugh when someone makes a joke.

- Laughs at others' jokes but seems confused at the same time.

- Gets talked into doing or saying silly or embarrassing things.

- Lets himself be bossed around by a group of students.

- Tattles on other students a lot, even though they deny they have done anything.

- May have difficulty explaining why he is tattling; it may be the result of a feeling that someone is being cruel rather than having concrete evidence.

Tips and Tricks for Managing Immaturity

- **Jokes are funny.** Attempt to explain to the student with Asperger's why jokes are funny. It may be tough—most jokes are no longer funny if you have to explain them. If this does not work, teach the student some jokes of his own to tell—and make sure he understands why they are funny.

- **Stock your classroom with age-appropriate joke and riddle books** and let the student with Asperger's take them home for assigned reading. When the books come back to class, ask her which jokes were her favorites and have her explain why.

- **What's popular.** Try to stay somewhat current with what is popular with students in your class, such as books, cartoons, video games, and music, so that when you hear references to pop culture, you will recognize them and can address them with the student who seems lost. (This will also help you recognize whether inappropriate conversations are going on in your classroom.)

- **Be the "cool" older kid.** If you have an opportunity to assign a student in your class to be a buddy for a younger class, your student with Asperger's may gain a lot from this experience by getting to be the "cool," older kid for a change.

- **Recognizing being "egged on."** If classmates are egging on embarrassing behavior in the student with Asperger's, gently explain that his classmates are not being kind and make them apologize. This is a hard thing to say when he thinks he is getting positive attention, so choose your words carefully. You can say things such as, "I do not think they are being good friends," or "I think that they are laughing for the wrong reasons."

- **Tattling can become a real problem with students with Asperger's.** Sometimes, they feel their sense of right and wrong has been ruffled, even if there is no major violation of rules. Or, they do not really know what exactly is going on, but they know their feelings are hurt, and someone needs to fix it—namely, you. If there is excessive tattling beyond the point where you want to hear both sides, you may need to make a list of rules for what is acceptable to tattle about, and post it in the classroom. Suggestions for what to put on the list could include when someone is getting hurt, when behavior is exceptionally mean and on purpose, or when something is unsafe. Things you could encourage students not to tattle about could include accidents or things that do not harm people. Do what works for your classroom as you make the list. Then, review the rules with your students and refer students to the list, making sure that tattlers follow the rules.

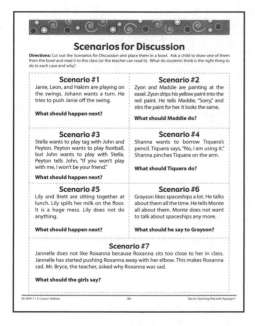

- **Scenarios for Discussion (page 98).** After your tattling discussion (above), have a class discussion to find out whether students can discern what the right thing to do is in different situations. Read a couple of the Scenarios for Discussion and discuss each one. What do students think is the right thing to do in each case and why?

Scenarios for Discussion

Directions: Cut out the Scenarios for Discussion and place them in a bowl. Ask a child to draw one of them from the bowl and read it to the class (or the teacher can read it). What do students think is the right thing to do in each case and why?

Scenario #1

Janie, Leon, and Hakim are playing on the swings. Johann wants a turn. He tries to push Janie off the swing.

What should happen next?

Scenario #2

Zyon and Maddie are painting at the easel. Zyon drips his yellow paint into the red paint. He tells Maddie, "Sorry," and stirs the paint for her. It looks the same.

What should Maddie do?

Scenario #3

Stella wants to play tag with John and Peyton. Peyton wants to play football, but John wants to play with Stella. Peyton tells John, "If you won't play with me, I won't be your friend."

What should happen next?

Scenario #4

Shanna wants to borrow Tiquera's pencil. Tiquera says, "No, I am using it." Shanna pinches Tiquera on the arm.

What should Tiquera do?

Scenario #5

Lily and Brett are sitting together at lunch. Lily spills her milk on the floor. It is a huge mess. Lily does not do anything.

What should happen next?

Scenario #6

Grayson likes spaceships a lot. He talks about them all the time. He tells Monte all about them. Monte does not want to talk about spaceships any more.

What should he say to Grayson?

Scenario #7

Jannelle does not like Roxanna because Roxanna sits too close to her in class. Jannelle has started pushing Roxanna away with her elbow. This makes Roxanna sad. Mr. Bryce, the teacher, asked why Roxanna was sad.

What should the girls say?

Inappropriate Behavior

The term "inappropriate behavior" covers a range of actions. For example, perhaps a student laughs when another student trips and falls, even though it is clear a classmate is hurt. Or, maybe a student continues laughing loudly five minutes after everyone else has stopped. It can even be very disruptive behavior, such as shouting at a classmate or running around the desks when she does not want to hand in a paper. Inappropriate behavior is anything that causes classmates to stare in amazement or to fear or dislike the student, or that disrupts the class. This is the behavior that teachers dread from any student. This often takes a great deal of time and energy to address and resolve.

Occasionally, students with Asperger's exhibit inappropriate behavior. Their tendency to react strongly to sensory input they cannot easily tolerate, as well as their difficulty with understanding social cues, can cause them to be disruptive in class. Below are ideas to look beyond the immediate behavior to find solutions.

Indicators of Inappropriate Behavior

- Shows inappropriate reactions (laughs at others getting hurt, gets angry at a simple mishap).

- Laughs, cries, yells, runs, or does other highly disruptive things, especially at the wrong times.

- Upsets, angers, or frightens classmates.

- Challenges teachers or other authority figures who try to manage their behavior.

Tips and Tricks for Managing Inappropriate Behavior

- **Gently call attention to behavior.** If the behavior is minor, such as laughing too long or loudly at a joke, gently call attention to it as you would for any other student. Say, "José, can you see that everyone else has stopped laughing?" Noticing that others have moved on should prompt him to move on too.

- **Have a private conversation.** If the student seems oblivious to gentle comparisons, talk to her privately. She may respond better to direct instruction about how to behave.

- **After you point out the inappropriate behavior, be prepared to police it.** Work out a silent signal with the student, such as shaking your head or putting a finger to your lips, to remind the student it is time to stop the behavior.

- **Videotape your classroom.** Show the student how he acts compared to his classmates. Be private about this; you do not want to ridicule the student or leave no room for natural differences. Be sure to provide positive examples of the student's behavior as well.

- **Be careful whom you seat together.** Some students feed off of each other's behavior. A student with Asperger's may be especially susceptible to another, more savvy student's encouragement to act out. Seat the student with Asperger's with students who are not likely to encourage inappropriate behavior.

- **Transitions are difficult for many students, but especially for students with Asperger's.** Try to build in a little extra time during transitions for students to get the wiggles out, calm down again, and get instructions from you about what is coming next.

- **Speaking of instructions, forewarned is forearmed.** If you are going to a special class or on a field trip, or even to lunch or the playground, remind students of the behavior you expect. Do not shy away from telling students you will be watching for specific things. Try to stay positive and explain what you will be watching for. For example, say, "Lauren will keep her hands on her own lunch," because you know she can do it.

- **Write it. Explain it. Demonstrate it.** We often use catch phrases such as, *Keep your hands to yourself* or *Worry about yourself*, but we rarely explain what those phrases mean. These phrases become very important when we talk to students about appropriate behavior. Every time you use one of these phrases in class, stop, write it on the board, and explain what it means while using demonstrations.

- **There are times a student may need to be removed from the situation.** If a student cannot control himself after a few warnings, remove him from the activity if you think it will help him calm down.

- **Be aware that some students will use disruptive behavior to avoid activities they do not like,** so in those cases, you will have to use means other than removing the student to discourage the behavior, such as removing him but sending the work along with him. Otherwise, you will have a student who misses every math lesson or every music class because he has learned to act out during those times.

- **If the inappropriate behavior gets very disruptive, remember to keep lines of communication open with parents and your principal.** Be aware of your school's policies about disruptive students and document every incident. Your first responsibility is to make sure that no one is hurt in your classroom, so follow your school's policies to make sure that this does not happen. Also, try to have an assistant or other teacher nearby to act as backup in case you need to remove the student.

- **Calm, compassionate, but firm approach.** Although it can be very trying to deal with a student who frequently exhibits disruptive or inappropriate behavior, use all the tricks you have up your sleeve not to lose your patience. Students will look to you as a role model, so it is best to show them that a calm, compassionate, but firm approach is ideal when dealing with a tricky situation in the classroom.

Inability to Build Friendships

This book has looked at many of the reasons students with Asperger's may have a hard time building friendships, such as immature behavior, difficulty carrying on conversations or reading body language. However, it has not yet met the issue of friendships head on. A good friend can make a huge difference in the life of a student. As a teacher, you may feel that helping a child develop friendships is a parent's responsibility, and of course it is, but you also know that when a tearful student comes to you on the playground with a friend problem, you need to have some kind words and helpful solutions ready for both students and parents. Students who feel alone or upset in your classroom will not learn as easily as those who feel like they have friends. For this reason, it is worth investing some time and effort into helping students get along, and even in helping them develop friendships. Here are some solutions that are geared toward students with Asperger's, but can apply to your other students as well.

Indicators of an Inability to Build Friendships

- Plays alone in most situations.

- Does not initiate play with others, at least not successfully.

- Does not greet classmates or tell them good-bye at the end of the day.

- Sits alone at lunch.

- Does not talk about playing with others outside of school.

- Receive notes or requests from parents to have conferences about unkind classmates.

Tips and Tricks for Managing an Inability to Build Friendships

- **Carefully consider the student's personality before you start trying to find friends for her.** Many students with Asperger's (and other students as well) truly prefer to play alone. While they may learn to feign interest in other's conversations and play in order to blend in, their actual preference could be solitude, and that is OK.

- **Use classroom seating to improve the student's chances for making friends.** Seat him next to a student who has common interests, who is well liked and outgoing, who seems to like the student, or who has a calm and engaging personality.

- **Pair students.** You can also pair students on projects or as reading buddies to see if a friendship will blossom as they get to know each other better.

- **Consult your school policy.** If parents are asking you about playmates and play dates, consult your school policy before handing out names and phone numbers for potential play dates.

- **Think twice before you set students up on play dates.** Elementary school students are not shy about offering their opinions about whom they do and do not want to play with. A play date rejection could make the situation worse.

- **Friendship workshop.** If students are not getting along, consider asking your school guidance counselor to do a friendship workshop.

- **Don't take sides.** Speaking of guidance counselors, it is often a good idea to ask a counselor to step in to handle friendship issues so that you do not get too involved in students' squabbles, but can instead remain neutral. If students perceive you as too involved, they may feel you are taking sides in a disagreement, and that undermines your ability to teach them and remain the authority figure in the classroom.

- **Encourage students to hang around each other** and not exclusively with you. You are the teacher, not the buddy.

- **Read books about friendship.** Students with Asperger's may have little idea of how friendships naturally blossom. Reading books about this can help. Stock your classroom with some of these examples:

    - *Friends* by Helme Heine (Aladdin, 1997);

    - *How to Be a Friend* by Laurie Krasny Brown (Little, Brown, 2001);

    - *Join In and Play* by Cheri J. Meiners (Free Spirit Publishing, 2003);

    - *Just a New Neighbor* by Gina and Mercer Mayer (Golden Books, 2000); and

    - *Will I Have a Friend?* by Miriam Cohen (Star Bright Books, 2009).

    Be sure to preview all books before you share them with the class to make sure they are a good fit.

- **Deal with that student's behavior on an individual basis.** Try not to punish the whole class for something a few students do wrong, because this can set up the student with Asperger's to be further ostracized. For example, if you have promised extra time on the playground, but have three or four students who are very disruptive, it might not be the best solution to punish the entire class by taking away the extra playground time. (Silent lunch is another common example of this.) This blanket punishment is something teachers often resort to in an attempt to make better-behaved classmates exert positive peer pressure on the few who misbehave. However, it rarely seems to work to control those few students, and in the case of a student with Asperger's, can end up unfairly singling him out if he truly cannot control some of his behaviors. It is usually better to deal with that student's behavior on an individual basis.

- **Sometimes, you may need to talk to parents about friendship situations.** If a student does not have many friends and parents request a meeting to find out why, this conversation can be uncomfortable. You can expect civility and mutual respect in your classroom, but you cannot force friendships to blossom. You also cannot really recommend behavioral changes that would improve the student's chances for making more friends. Your best bet is to talk about how well the student follows the classroom rules: no bullying, being kind, using kind words, etc. If the parent is unaware of the student's social issues, you should consult the guidance counselor and ask her to sit in on the meeting to make sure you use appropriate language and address the right topics.

Argumentative Behavior

Every teacher has had at least one student who argues. For most students, this is just a means to try to gain control or get something they want. This is not necessarily the case for the student with Asperger's. Because, in his mind, many issues have a right and wrong answer, if he thinks his answer is the right one, he will probably argue his point. Compromise and negotiation are not usually strong suits for students with Asperger's, so be prepared to be challenged. Here are some ideas for how to handle the student who argues with you. For more information, see page 78 about Inflexibility or Rigid Thinking.

Indicators of Being Argumentative

- Cannot take no for an answer.

- Will not let things go, even when you try to distract her or end the discussion.

- Brings up (often with great accuracy) past events or conversations to prove a point.

- Follows logical lines of reasoning with little regard for whether others are getting upset or frustrated with a discussion.

- Does not acknowledge a clear attempt to assert authority and end a conversation. For example, "Because I am the teacher, and I said so."

Tips and Tricks for Dealing with an Argumentative Student

- **Remind yourself frequently that the student may not be trying to be difficult on purpose.** Both teachers and parents commonly mention that students with Asperger's seem reluctant to follow simple directions. This reluctance to get started on a task has been referred to as inertia. Inertia can lead to a seemingly endless stream of excuses and arguments from a student as to why he is not responding. Students' reasoning (or seeming lack of it) can be frustrating, but it may simply be part of their makeup and not a deliberate intent to challenge you.

- **Be careful to set a tone of authority early on in your classroom.** Although you certainly want to hear students' side of things, you do not want to get caught up in endless negotiations with any student. It sets a precedent for other students to try their hand at arguing with you as well.

- **Write down the class rules and post them in your classroom.** It is harder to argue with a written document. But, once you post rules, be prepared to follow them to the letter, because you are putting them in writing. Breaking the written rules would be another reason for the student to argue with you.

- **Limit the number of exchanges.** If a student does start an argument, limit the number of exchanges to two "volleys." Cutting the student off at a specific number gives her less time to get wound up.

> **CLASS RULES**
>
> **Rule 1:**
> Be kind to others.
>
> **Rule 2:**
> Respect your classmates, your teacher, and your school.
>
> **Rule 3:**
> Listen carefully.
>
> **Rule 4:**
> Follow directions.
>
> **Rule 5:**
> Be safe.

- **Write or draw the argument.** If a student seems like he just needs to have the last word, have him write down his reasoning or draw a picture of the point he wants to argue. Explain that you will discuss it with him later. Hopefully, when the time comes to do so, some of the urgency will have diminished.

- **Think about whether you are arguing about fact or opinion and act accordingly.** You can postpone a factual disagreement until you can look it up and point to the facts in print. If there is a disagreement of opinions, you can agree to disagree or table the discussion until later. Just remind the student that you are the teacher, and you are therefore in charge, so you get to make the decision.

- **Acknowledge the argument the student is making without giving in.** You can say, "I understand your point of view, even if I cannot agree with you."

- **Students should understand the difference between disagreeing with you and being disrespectful.** It is one thing for a student to think that the main idea in a book is something other than what you think it is, and another for a student to shout his opinion at you. If you have to speak to a student about his actions during a disagreement, make sure it is for being disrespectful and not just for having a different opinion.

- **If two students are arguing, you will need to draw the line at an appropriate point.** Sometimes, healthy discussion is a good thing. It makes students think. However, early elementary students usually do not have enough self-control to manage a reasonable discussion for very long before someone gets angry or cries. Know when to step in and say that enough is enough.

- **If a student gets very agitated, it may be best to remove her to the guidance office to cool off.** An angry, arguing student is hard to control, and if you are the person she is arguing with, having a third party intervene will let you remain in control of the rest of the class.

- **Finally, remember that this student may need to see the big picture more than others.** It is often enough to tell students what to do and expect them to do it, because you are the teacher and they are the students. But, a student with Asperger's may need to see how your directions fit into the scheme of things to understand the "why" of what you are telling him to do. If you offer an explanation to begin with, you may be able to head off the argument before it even starts.

Being a Target of Bullying

Students with Asperger's are often targets of bullying. Others can easily make fun of them if they have unusual behaviors or social skills. It can be hard for teachers, parents, and even sympathetic students to watch classmates gang up on one student. However, you should treat this situation like you would treat any other bullying situation—with zero tolerance, according to your school's policy on bullying.

Indicators of Being a Target of Bullying

- Seems fearful, angry, or sad, or cries often but does not say why.

- Avoids certain classmates.

- Dreads lunch, recess, or other less supervised times.

- Asks to be excused from a certain special class, such as PE.

- Misses school often.

- Claims to lose lunch money or other possessions.

Tips and Tricks for Improving a Bullying Situation

- **First of all, set a good example.** It is easy to use sarcasm when you are having a frustrating day, or fire off an impatient comment at a student. Your mood sets the tone in your classroom, so listen to yourself to know what your classroom feels like for students.

- **Be aware of what is happening with your students.** If you suspect bullying is going on in your classroom, watch and listen to conversations and actions on the playground, in the lunchroom, in hallways, at restroom doors, and in corners of the classroom. Ask other teachers to watch out for incidents during art, music, and PE classes as well. You cannot be everywhere or see everything, but often, if you are looking for something, you will find it.

- **Remember that bullying is not just done with fists. It is also done with words.** "If you do not do what I tell you to do, I will not be your friend," is bullying, just the same as hitting or kicking. (Many school systems define an incident as bullying only if it is a repeated incident, so be aware of how your school defines it before talking to students about it.)

- **Is This Bullying Behavior? worksheet (page 108).** If you suspect bullying in your classroom, announce to the class that you are always on the lookout for signs of bullying. Explain what bullying is and give examples. Use the Is This Bullying Behavior? worksheet to show examples of bullying. Go over it together as a class if you do not have strong readers or let individual students or small groups work on it together. The worksheet is a trick; all of the scenarios are potential examples of bullying. (Note: All school systems define bullying differently, so you should check the worksheet against your school's policy to make sure the scenarios fit with your school's definition. For more information, visit stopbullying.gov.)

- **Document everything you find out from your observations.** Include names, dates, what led up to each incident, who was involved, and how you handled it, even if you decided to let things play out. (Sometimes, it is best to let students solve things. That can be an active solution by a teacher.)

- **Remind students that if someone is bullying them, they should come to you and talk in private.** Tell them they can write you a note, get a parent to call, or tell you a secret.

- **Often, instead of confronting the bully, removing the opportunity is a good option.** Instead of protecting the target, start shadowing (or have your assistant shadow) the bully more than usual. If he discovers you are watching him constantly, he may get frustrated with all the attention and get discouraged from bullying others.

- **If you decide to confront a student whom you suspect of bullying, expect her to deny everything.** Have specific questions ready for her. Do not ask, "Shannon, are you being mean to Lakshmi?" Instead, say, "Shannon, I saw you push Lakshmi at the water fountain. Why did you think it was OK to do that?"

- **Encourage kindness in your classroom by getting students to write on a "Kind Things" board.** Post a large sheet of bulletin board paper in your classroom. Write students' names on two sets of index card-sized self-stick notes. Give each student two classmates' names. Instruct students to write kind things about each classmate on the notes and sign their names. Preview what each student wrote and then post the notes on the Kind Things board for the whole class to read.

- **Celebrate what students have in common.** Get students together in small groups to talk about favorite sports, kinds of pets, places they went on vacation, favorite video games, favorite hobbies, and favorite school subjects. Move students around every few minutes or so to talk to new friends based on new things they have in common.

- **Role-play how to talk to bullies to help students think about what they would say in different situations.** Let students share their answers with the class. Try to choose students who tend to have funny, snappy comebacks that diffuse situations so that students with Asperger's have examples for how to reply back in effective ways when being teased. You may need to do a little extra role-playing with the student with Asperger's so that the tone sounds natural when he uses one of the comebacks.

- **Foster alliances in your classroom.** If you have students who are being targeted by the same classmate, seat the "targets" together, along with some mature students who are likely to be kind and offer a buffer. Give these seatmates a chance to be friends and to become a force for good in the classroom.

- **Be careful.** If you do have a student with Asperger's who is a target of other students, be careful how you stand up for her. In some cases, coming to her rescue may stop others' behavior toward her at that moment, but may instead make her a bigger target at a future time when you are not around to intervene.

- **Report according to your school and district policy.** If any instances of bullying go beyond a little teasing, happen more than once, or seem like they could easily escalate, document them carefully and report them according to your school and district policy. The most important thing is to make sure your students are safe.

Is This Bullying Behavior?

Directions: Read each sentence. If you think each paragraph tells about a kind of bullying, circle the word **Yes**. If you think it is not bullying, circle the word **No**.

1. Maggie wanted to get the seat in the very back of the bus. She grabbed Connor's shirt and pulled him out of the seat and onto the floor.

   Is this bullying?   **Yes**   **No**

2. Denetia told her teacher that Ray took her pencil, but he didn't. Ray got in trouble.

   Is this bullying?   **Yes**   **No**

3. Three girls hit Caroline and took her sweater.

   Is this bullying?   **Yes**   **No**

4. Monte used sidewalk chalk to write mean things about Erika on the school sidewalk. Everyone in her class saw it.

   Is this bullying?   **Yes**   **No**

5. Dave and Yong told Spence that they would not be his friend unless he stopped playing with Carlton.

   Is this bullying?   **Yes**   **No**

6. When Selina got glasses, Ally and Tim said she looked weird and called her "big-eyes."

   Is this bullying?   **Yes**   **No**

7. In the lunchroom, Johanna told Mike that if he didn't give up his candy bar, she would throw his whole lunch box in the trash.

   Is this bullying?   **Yes**   **No**

8. Trejan wanted to play basketball on the playground, but the other boys told him that they did not want him to play, and he should go away.

   Is this bullying?   **Yes**   **No**

Personal Responsibility

Many people think of personal responsibility as something preschoolers start learning when they are in class, something kindergartners have to learn when they enter "big school" from preschool, or especially, something that only parents should teach. However, personal responsibility is something students are still learning through all stages of school. Being responsible for one's own work and for one's self can be tough for many students, and especially for those with Asperger's. Often, when parents and teachers are aware that a student is "different," they expect less independence from the student even when he is capable of more. This can hinder the student from developing important self-help skills and responsibility he desperately needs for school and for life. Young students need to be able to open their lunch food containers and deal with their personal needs, such as toileting. As students get older, they become responsible for so much more: school papers, projects, permission slips, and other deadlines. Parents and teachers can use these ideas to work together to help students with Asperger's (and their neurotypical classmates) learn to tackle self-help skills and be more responsible.

Trouble with Following Directions and Rules

Following directions can be difficult for all students for many reasons. Some cannot pay attention long enough to hear you and then process what you said. Some have language retention or processing problems. Some can follow oral directions well, but cannot read well enough to follow written directions. If you add Asperger's syndrome into the mix, then you also may add resistance to change, especially if you are asking a student to follow directions for new rules or a new way of doing things.

Indicators of Trouble with Following Directions and Rules

- Does not finish tasks.

- Argues with you about directions.

- Does this the old way, even if you clearly stated you wanted students to do things differently.

- Stops at the point where the directions change.

- Gets answers wrong. (This would apply in math, for example, where you are teaching a new math skill.)

Tips and Tricks for Trouble with Following Directions and Rules

- **Get students' full attention and eye contact.** Before you give any directions, make sure you have students' full attention and eye contact. If the student with Asperger's is reluctant to make eye contact with you, stand near her seat to give her the best chance for listening while giving the directions to the rest of the class.

- **Use a microphone.** If your school offers the technology, give all instructions over a microphone that works with surround sound. This can help students pay better attention and can also help with auditory processing problems.

- **Work out a signal** such as ringing a bell, turning off lights, or blowing a whistle when students need to listen for instructions.

- **Use hand motions to make visual cues for students as you talk.** For example, if you want a student to collect the class homework, as you ask her to do so, pick up one student's homework and hold it up so she has a visual as well as a verbal cue to follow.

- **Have students repeat directions back to you,** especially if someone seems unsure of what to do next. Ask different students to repeat directions each time; you should not always single out the student with Asperger's. It benefits her to hear the directions repeated by others, just as it benefits her to say them herself.

- **Repeat multistep directions.** If you are using multistep directions, repeat the steps as students get close to finishing each step. For example, say, "Now that you are almost finished with coloring your picture, you may start cutting it out." This serves as a reminder for what students should be doing if they are getting off task and lets them know where they should be in the process.

- **Make your directions age appropriate for students.** Give short directions for younger students and longer ones for older students.

- **Show work in completed stages.** At each point in your directions, show work in completed stages, so that students know what they are working toward.

- **Give students written or picture copies of the directions you want them to follow.** This will prevent them from arguing with you later on about what exactly you had said.

- **Directions become rules.** Any time you give directions for something that you do every day, be aware you are establishing a norm in your classroom, and these directions become rules. Any time you deviate from the rules, you are changing the game for students. Some will adapt easily, and some will not. If you do things differently next time, your student with Asperger's, as well as other students, may see this as a mistake or inconsistency and have a hard time changing gears.

- **Think carefully about your teaching style.** Following this, be aware of your own teaching style. Are you rigid, nicely flexible, or loose with following the rules you have established? Think carefully about your teaching style and how you might need to modify it to best suit all of the students in your classroom. Students cannot easily follow the rules if you are constantly relaxing or changing them.

- **Post classroom rules in a prominent place** so that all students can follow them. Consult the rules chart when there is a question. Do not make exceptions except in extreme circumstances.

- **Before you post the rules, make sure that they are reasonable and build in some flexibility.** For example, if you write a rule such as *Students may take a restroom break at 10:00*, it is possible that a student with Asperger's will have an accident in your classroom because he is following the rules by not asking to go sooner, no matter how much orange juice he drank at breakfast. Be sure to explain that there can be exceptions to rules, or rewrite the rule to say *All students may take a restroom break at 10:00. Students may ask to go to the restroom before 10:00 if necessary.*

- **Any time the rules are going to change, do not spring it on your student with Asperger's.** Heading off frustration can be as simple as saying, "Today, we are changing the rules." Be prepared to give a logical explanation for why the rules are changing, even if it is just, "Because I am the teacher, and I am in charge."

- **As stated earlier in this book, you can also blame changing the rules on a higher authority.** If your principal has decided that no one is allowed to climb on the largest piece of playground equipment until the slide is attached more securely, then you can use her authority as an excuse. She changed the rules, not you. The student cannot argue with her, so he has no choice but to follow the new rule.

Easily Overwhelmed with Large Tasks

As students get older, schoolwork becomes harder, and students are faced with doing projects that last for several days. These projects are simple at first and become harder with each grade level. All students face becoming overwhelmed with what looks like a ton of work at first glance, but when broken into smaller tasks, it can be more easily managed. As you assign hard work that takes longer amounts of time, here is how to help students navigate it.

Indicators of Being Easily Overwhelmed with Large Tasks

- Does not turn in some or all parts of his work.

- Turns in work late.

- Loses assignments.

- Gets overwhelmed with projects.

- Parents report frustration with projects.

- Work is sloppy or disorganized.

Tips and Tricks for Improving Being Easily Overwhelmed with Large Tasks

- **Explain to parents at the beginning of the year what their roles are in their children's work.** This is actually helpful to all parents because you will have a range of amounts of help from parents—from not ever reading their children's assignments to doing everything for their children. It may even help to send home a note with a sample project that lists what students should do and the maximum parents should do, with an explanation that the idea is for students to do as much of their own work as possible. For example, you might want to explain that parents can help with arranging items in a folder, point out spelling mistakes, type on a computer, and help navigate to appropriate computer sites, but that students should do all of their own writing and drawing.

- **Project Planner worksheet (page 114).** When you send home a first project, teach scheduling along with it. Don't just break it into small steps, but assign due dates for those small steps. Use the Project Planner worksheet for students and parents so that they have project steps and due dates summarized and all in one place for reference.

- **Calendars.** If the student with Asperger's prefers calendars, send home a calendar page with the small due dates on them so that students have a visual reference for project deadlines.

- **Multiple due dates.** Do not ask for the entire project to be turned in on one day. Instead, ask to see each smaller task on its own individual due date.

Name:		
Project Planner for		
Step 1	**What You Need to Do**	**Step 1 Due Date**
Step 2	**What You Need to Do**	**Step 2 Due Date**
Step 3	**What You Need to Do**	**Step 3 Due Date**
Step 4	**What You Need to Do**	**Step 4 Due Date**
Step 5	**What You Need to Do**	**Step 5 Due Date**
Step 6	**What You Need to Do**	**Step 6 Due Date**

- **Disorganization.** Many students with Asperger's have particular difficulty staying organized. (See Disorganization on page 115 for more about this topic.) Designate a place for students to store project work in the classroom. For example, purchase a set of inexpensive cardboard file folders or a mailbox-style organizer and let students keep parts of their projects there as they complete them.

- **Resisting or refusing to do a project.** If the project you assigned does not interest the student with Asperger's, he may resist or even refuse to do it for this reason. You will simply have to talk him into it. The student is going to have to do some work that is not in the comfort zone of his favorite subject, even if he sees no value in it. Explain that all students have to do work they do not like to do from time to time, and you have the same rules and expectations for him as you do for all other students.

- **Allow a time for this student to shine with a project.** If the student has a favorite topic, let him choose it as the focus for the next project. You are likely to see amazing results and true dedication to the work when he has some choice in the subject matter. One way to do this is to add a flexible piece to an existing core project. For example, if the project is a report about your state, let each student draw a map or build a model of his favorite place to visit. You can bet your student with Asperger's who loves roller coasters will work extra hard on his model of one.

Project Planner for _____

Step 1	What You Need to Do	Step 1 Due Date
Step 2	What You Need to Do	Step 2 Due Date
Step 3	What You Need to Do	Step 3 Due Date
Step 4	What You Need to Do	Step 4 Due Date
Step 5	What You Need to Do	Step 5 Due Date
Step 6	What You Need to Do	Step 6 Due Date

Disorganization

Students with Asperger's often struggle with disorganization. Completing projects, managing papers, remembering where they put things, keeping their desks clean—all of these things can be problems for students with Asperger's. They can get so distracted with the small things that they cannot focus on the larger issues, such as making a clean space to work in, actually finishing a paper, or getting that note signed and then returning it. Teachers and parents must work together to help them tackle this problem. Because many students suffer from disorganization, these techniques can impart a useful life skill for all of them.

Indicators of Disorganization

- Has a messy desk, backpack, or lunch box.

- Keeps papers much longer than they are needed.

- Does not return important papers or homework on time, if at all.

- Library books do not go home or do not come back to school.

- Tries to carry everything in his hands, and so frequently puts down objects and loses them.

- Puts things "in a safe place," only to forget where that place is.

- Cannot clean up unless you break the job into small tasks.

- Cannot complete projects.

- Is forgetful; parents often come to school to deliver forgotten work.

Tips and Tricks for Disorganization

- **Start with you. Look closely at areas of your classroom to see if you are really keeping it clutter-free.** Revisit the section on pages 12–14 about how to organize your classroom for a student with Asperger's. If your classroom is very cluttered or disorganized, you may be overwhelming this student so that she cannot keep on top of her own mess. At the very least, you should periodically purge clutter to set a good example. You do not have to organize what you do not keep!

- **Make students share responsibility** for the upkeep of the classroom by having cleanup time. Assign each student a job to do. Consistently rotate who does what so that everyone has an important cleanup task.

- **Keep only what you need.** To address clutter and disorganization with classroom materials, consider keeping a pencil or materials box at your desk instead of letting the student keep it inside of his desk. Let him get only the materials that he needs.

- **Send home a monthly or weekly calendar** with upcoming important dates such as school assignments, field trips, and other things parents can help students remember. Copy it on the same color of bright paper each time.

- **Send home reminders for permission slips** that need to be signed and returned. Copy them on the same color of bright paper each time.

- **Email vs. notes sent home.** If you need students to return items to school and find that the items do not come back consistently, forgo sending notes home and send emails to parents because they may be unlikely to get the written notes anyway.

- **Color code folders to help students keep up with homework.** Keep math in the pink folder, spelling in the red folder, writing in the blue folder, etc. Do not worry about copying homework papers on colored paper because that can get expensive. Just use a highlighter to make a colored swipe across the top of each student's paper, and that will tell her what folder to file it in. If you do not want to use separate folders, use colored tabs in a notebook.

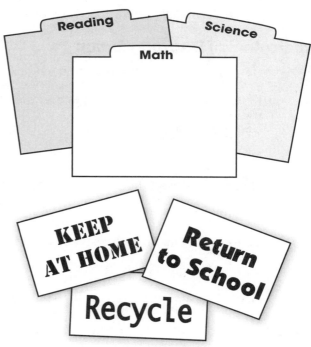

- **A stamping system.** To solve the problem of hoarding papers, review what should go home, what should come back to school, and what should stay at home to be recycled each day. If possible, use a stamping system and mark papers Keep at Home, Return to School, and Recycle.

- **Share whatever organizational system you use with parents so that they can reinforce its use at home.** For example, if you do use color-coded folders, parents can ask, "Did you put your math paper in your pink folder?"

- **Start each day with a morning checklist of things to do and personalize it for your classroom.** Disorganization does not only manifest itself in clutter and papers. It also shows up in completing assignments. Students often have a hard time finishing work, not just because they cannot find it, but because they cannot organize tasks. Items to check off might include *put your coat and lunch box away*, *turn in your homework folder*, *check the board for an assignment*, and *sharpen your pencils*. Laminate the list and use a write-on/wipe-away marker to help the student fill it in each day. If the student is more visual, add pictures to the list.

A Great Way to Start the Day!

☑ Hang up your coat.

☑ Put your lunch box away.

☑ Turn in your homework.

☑ Check the board for new assignments.

☑ Sharpen your pencils.

- **Give older students a chance to use an assignment book or date book.** For elementary age students, often a book that is 8 ½" x 11" with a full month on each page is a good size because it is harder to lose and shows several weeks at a time. Partner with parents to stay on top of upcoming project dates. If you do not want to suggest that students use a date book, or if you want more control over filling out the due dates for the class, copy the blank calendar found on page 118 and fill in the dates yourself, along with due dates.

- **Color coding their date books to match their color-coded folders** is something that highly visual students might enjoy. They may want to highlight their math assignments in pink, their spelling tests in red, etc. Try to let students with Asperger's use colored pencils with erasers, because they are sure to want to erase any mistakes.

- **Review the previous section, Easily Overwhelmed with Large Tasks** (pages 112–113), for more ideas about how to help students get through projects beyond their normal homework.

The Month of ___

Sunday	Monday	Tuesday	Wednesday	Thursday	Friday	Saturday

Tips for Teaching Kids with Asperger's

Trouble Retaining Information

If you are several weeks into the school year, and you have one student who still cannot remember how to pay for school lunch despite your repeated instructions, then that student may have trouble retaining information. Then, he pays for his lunch every day and you are sure that he's "got it." But the next day, he seems unsure once again and has to ask for help. What's going on?

This is actually a common problem for many students, not just those with Asperger's. For the student with Asperger's, several things may be going on. The student may be experiencing sensory overload at the time that he needs to recall the information. The student may be resistant to the information because he does not see the logic in the procedure, or he may simply be busy with his favorite subject at the moment. Try some of the ideas below to see if you can break through whatever wall is there to get him to remember how to complete his daily tasks without constant reminders.

Indicators of Trouble Retaining Information

- Shows no indication that it is time to do an everyday task.

- Acts like she is doing something for the first time every time.

- Cannot follow a routine that the rest of the class has mastered.

- Seems unengaged with the environment around him when others are learning to do something.

- Has trouble navigating familiar routes; cannot be the line leader to the gym or playground even after a few weeks at school without plenty of help getting there.

- Constantly watches classmates for cues for what to do.

- Cannot remember academic tasks and seems to have no foundation to build on for things such as sight words, math facts, spelling patterns, and book series.

- When you retell a story or a joke, other students will stop you and say, "I know!" This student does not do that.

Tips and Tricks for Trouble Retaining Information

- **Start the year by having lessons for how you do things.** Remind yourself that even if you are an old pro of a teacher, your way of doing things is completely new to your students. Do not hit the ground running with lessons, but take a couple of days to introduce them to the class, each other, and to you. This is hard to do with so much to cram into an academic year, but it will pay off in the long run as you find yourself having to repeat things fewer times.

- **Stick to routines as much as possible** and do not deviate from them until students get to know them well.

- **Post pictures of your most common routines in the areas where students will do them.** For example, post pictures of how students should sharpen pencils, wash hands, and get their folders. Also, post reminders where they are most needed, such as a sign next to the door that asks, "Do you have your coat?"

- **Introduce new faces many times,** especially to young students. For example, as students meet the PE teacher, say, "Class, this is Mr. Hicks." At the next PE class, say, "Do you remember Mr. Hicks?" When you see him in the hallway, greet him by saying, "Class, here is Mr. Hicks! Say hello to your PE teacher!" Students have a lot of new faces to master, so be sure to give them plenty of chances to do so.

- **Ask specific questions about the routine** you are currently tackling to help remind students what comes next, and anticipate their questions.

- **Learn with music.** It may feel silly, but students and adults remember important information better if it is set to music. If you are trying to get students to remember days of the week, their specials schedule, or the names of their classmates, sing a silly song about it and practice it daily with students. You will hear them singing the song to themselves as they try to remember the information.

- **Songs work with directions too.** Try singing a song that contains the directions to the office or cafeteria to help students remember how to find these places. Having a song to sing will take some of the fear out of walking to a new place.

- **Use a mnemonic device, a poem, or a rap** to help students remember important information if singing is not your style.

- **Listen to yourself as you give out information.** Do you get to the point quickly, or do you go on and on? Try to get to the point while students are still listening.

- **Make reasonable adjustments for a student who truly has difficulty with internalizing routines and retaining other information.** For example, if this student has trouble signing himself in and out as a car rider in the morning and a bus rider in the afternoon, consider prompting him to answer instead of expecting him to do it himself. In academic areas, if the student has an official diagnosis of Asperger's, talk to the school guidance counselor and curriculum coordinator to see whether some exceptions can be made. For example, if he cannot remember ten spelling words, see whether you can cut his list down to five. Be as flexible and positive as possible and be creative as you work with the student to help him be more successful.

- **Because people with Asperger's frequently have trouble sleeping and difficulty eating well,** it may be a struggle for them to maintain their focus through the day. If you suspect this is the case, send home a request for parents to fill out a list of the student's exact daily schedule, including mealtimes and bedtimes. Ask the student to verify the information and describe what she is eating for meals. If you see that the student is not sleeping enough or getting adequate nutrition, talk to your school guidance counselor to see what steps might be taken to help the student and her family address these issues.

Inability to Sit Still

Every teacher has several students who bring the image of "spaghetti in a chair" to mind. Preschool teachers of students as young as age two start working on sitting still for longer and longer times, and it is not an easy skill for many students to master. Having the "wiggles" can indicate many things, including being bored, not having had enough exercise for the day, being tired, being hot or cold, or simply being ready to move on to something else.

The fact is that society as a whole expects students to sit still for longer periods at earlier ages in school, but not at any other time. Family meals are shorter, more time is spent sitting in front of the TV or video games (which is not the same as sitting still and paying attention to something), and less time is spent in focused activities. So, many students only sit still and focus at school and have had little practice at it. Add to that the sensory stimulation needed by many students with Asperger's in order for them to focus, and you have many factors working against them that prevent them from doing anything but being in perpetual motion. You may have to address both the tendency not to sit still and the tendency to need additional stimulation such as deep pressure (from a weighted vest) to help students with Asperger's sit still and focus on learning.

Indicators of an Inability to Sit Still

- Rolls around on the floor, rocks in chair, flaps arms, or engages in any other repetitive motion that distracts himself or others.

- Bothers classmates with motions during learning time.

- Gets out of his chair at inappropriate times.

- Makes faces or noises.

- Fidgets—picks at clothing, scabs, hair, or other body parts.

- Makes mouth noises.

- Touches nearby objects.

- Uses elbows to crowd friends.

Tips and Tricks for an Inability to Sit Still

- **Plan tasks that require a lot of listening and concentration for the morning,** when students are still fresh and are not hungry.

- **"Please sit up in your seat," is a command often used, but you may want to demonstrate what that means.** Show students the difference between sitting up in a chair and slouching, so they can copy you and will know what to do when you ask them to sit up. Sitting up prevents leaning and therefore allows less wiggling.

- **Some students need more movement, rather than less, to pay attention.** Provide a few small exercise balls for students to sit on. The movements they have to make to stay on top of it will help them have just enough motion to pay attention to you. Make sure others get turns so it is not just the student with Asperger's who gets the special seat. (This special seat is great for building core muscles too.)

- **Use interaction to call back students who are drifting away.** Say things such as, "What other word looks like *ship*? Callie, can you answer that question?" Callie will be forced to participate for a minute, and therefore she will have to pay attention. To double the effect, call on her again a few minutes later.

- **Give the student with Asperger's something sensory yet unobtrusive to help him focus.** Something as simple as a piece of sandpaper to rub while you are talking may help him focus better. If the problem is keeping his hands to himself, giving the student something to hold, like the sandpaper, can also keep his hands busy.

- **Bear in mind that some students are naturally more social and require more interaction to learn well**, while others prefer to mull things over in silence. Try to allot for their preferences and learning styles by having designated times where students are allowed to be out of their seats.

- **Turn the tables and ask students to teach you about sitting still.** Show them what squirming looks like and ask them to model how to sit still for you. Give a small prize such as stickers to the student who does the best job.

- **If the student with Asperger's will respond to it, develop a nonverbal signal to let him know when he is wiggling too much,** such as shaking your head or gently squeezing his shoulder, or even wiggling back at him if you can do it without distracting the class. This will be especially helpful to students who do not realize they are moving.

- **If your school allows gum, let the student with Asperger's chew gum or eat hard candy to add some sensory stimulation.** This may decrease the need to move.

- **Who is Sitting Still? activity page 123.** Remember that for students with Asperger's, sitting still and paying attention during group activities is truly difficult, so exercise patience and help them learn a measure of self-control and to recognize when they are not paying attention or sitting still.

- **Finally, remember that all students need frequent wiggle breaks!** Build in movement during transition times and take advantage of all the playground time you can so that students have outlets for their need to use their large muscle groups.

Who is Sitting Still?

Directions: Circle the students who are sitting quietly. What are the other students doing? Tell your teacher about it.

Inability to Stay on Task

Starting as early as late preschool, teachers start training students to focus on their work for longer and longer stretches. By early kindergarten, students need to be able to do at least 10 minutes of desk work at a time or listen attentively to a story. By the end of first grade, that time has expanded to 20 minutes. This is a fairly long time to expect a seven-year-old to pay attention, but it is part of the norm for elementary school. By the end of third grade, students face their first standardized tests. Some students are ready to sit still, listen, and absorb information, while many others are not. Unless they are participating in hands-on learning, their focus wanders quickly.

Students with Asperger's may resort to self-soothing behavior (talking to themselves, making repetitive noises or motions) when they get bored or stressed during testing. Their teachers must keep them engaged so they complete their work successfully and allow their classmates to do the same. Here are some simple tricks for keeping students with Asperger's, as well as other students, engaged in their work.

Indicators of Inability to Stay on Task

- Moves around much more than necessary during quiet work time; falls off chair or rocks chair or desk.

- Drops materials.

- Bothers seatmates by talking to them or touching them.

- Does not finish work when others are finished long before.

- Completes work, but it looks rushed and messy as if the student waited until the last possible second to do it.

- Finds ways to interrupt himself: asks for tissues, needs to visit the restroom, sharpens pencils, throws away trash, etc.

Tips and Tricks for Inability to Stay on Task

- **Ideally, work on complicated desk work in the morning,** before students are tired and hungry.

- **Intersperse desk work with busier, noisier activities,** so that there is time in between for students to get a break from sitting still and being quiet.

- **Remember that adults get frequent bathroom and water breaks, and so should students.** Schedule time for breaks so that students know they will be getting a break and will not pester you for time out of the classroom during quiet work time.

- **If you have a particular student who has a hard time settling in to work,** sit near that student or have an assistant or volunteer sit near her so that she is less likely to misbehave. If you cannot put an adult near the student, seat her near quiet classmates. If she is still disruptive, move her seat to a quiet corner where she will have fewer distractions.

- **If students tend to encroach on each other's space** while sitting together, push desks slightly apart during desk work. Mark space on tables with masking tape.

- **If students share supplies for a project, make sure you have plenty of everything available for them to use.** This prevents fighting over the yellow crayon or the one pair of scissors.

- **Some students get discouraged and give up if they do not understand assignments.** Walk around frequently and quietly answer any questions that come up. Or, invite one student at a time to come quietly to your desk with any specific questions.

- **Try pairing students with partners to work on desk work.** This will give them a break from always working silently. Plus, you can pair students who can help each other in different ways. Pair a shy student with a gregarious student who is a potential friend, or a student who needs help with schoolwork with one of the brighter students in class. Pair a student who is weak in math with another who is strong in math. Pair the student with Asperger's with someone who is likely to work well with her as well.

- **Give some power to students.** Because desk work is not likely to be very exciting all of the time, poll your class to find out what they like to work on. Maybe some students enjoy mazes, while others love to cut and paste. Or, maybe you have a student who loves dolphins and another who plays pirates on the playground every day. You can always be flexible and create skill-based desk work that is more appealing because it caters somewhat to students' interests. And, if you have a student with Asperger's who has a favorite topic, that student may be quite excited to work on math word problems based on his favorite topic.

- **Desk Work Rules (page 126).** Give students copies of the Desk Work Rules worksheet to color and keep at their desks. Post the Desk Work Rules in the classroom and review the rules with students whenever they seem to need to hear them. If you find students are not behaving when they are working at their desks, copy the rules, laminate them, and attach copies to their desks as a daily reminder for what you expect out of them each day.

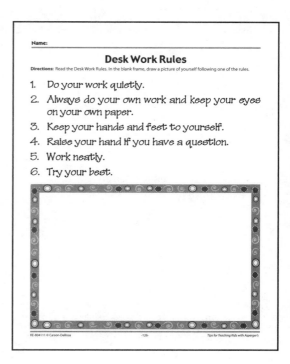

Desk Work Rules

Directions: Read the Desk Work Rules. In the blank frame, draw a picture of yourself following one of the rules.

1. Do your work quietly.
2. Always do your own work and keep your eyes on your own paper.
3. Keep your hands and feet to yourself.
4. Raise your hand if you have a question.
5. Work neatly.
6. Try your best.

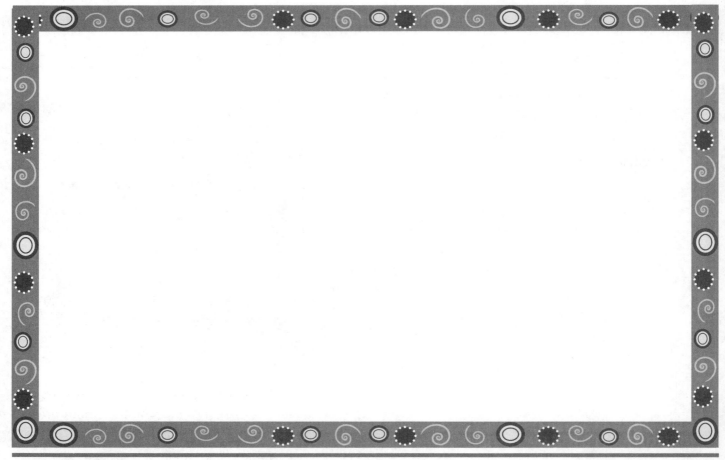

Difficulty Pacing Themselves

Students with Asperger's have two types of problems when it comes to pacing themselves and getting through their work. Sometimes, they speed through their work because they find it too hard and overwhelming. Other times, they are so meticulous about it that they can get about one problem done every fifteen minutes—they are too busy trying to write the perfect zero or include every last detail to actually solve more than one math problem. Both of these are issues students need to fix, because they will cause problems in testing, in upper grades, and in the workplace later on.

Indicators of Difficulty Pacing Themselves

- Work is sloppy, incomplete, and finished well before classmates.

- Work is complete, but thoughts seem half-finished or do not make sense.

- Work is barely done but may be erased a lot.

- Work is barely done but extremely neat.

- Work is incomplete but extremely detailed.

Tips and Tricks for Difficulty Pacing Themselves

- **Silent, color-coded timer.** Watches seem like a great idea, but often the ticking or the feel of wearing them are highly irritating to students with Asperger's. Instead, buy a silent, color-coded timer to help the student pace himself.

- **A timer works for both kinds of pacing issues,** for both schoolwork and things such as getting dressed (a tip for parents). For example, if you set the timer on five minutes, you can tell the student he must use all five minutes or that he only has five minutes.

- **Tell students how long things should take.** Often they have no idea. This is especially helpful for beginning readers.

- **Hold a student's hasty, messy paper at arm's length from her face.** If she cannot read it, it's too sloppy, and she needs to write more neatly. She may get the idea that it takes less time to do it if she does it right the first time. (Rather than have her erase each answer, you may want to let the student copy over the work, because erasing may be even more frustrating and take more time. Plus, doing a second copy reinforces the idea of drafting.)

- **Break assignments into smaller tasks.** Students who take too long may do better if you break things up into smaller tasks for them. Give assignments in smaller chunks so that they are not overwhelmed.

- **Slow down.** If you are hurrying, students will hurry. Pace yourself, and they will pace themselves too, because they won't feel rushed.

- **If there is extra time, make students check their work.** Be sure you show them how to check work. Explain that they should reread questions and their answers, check spelling, and redo their math, etc.

- **Show students how to add more to their answers.** Don't say, "Can you?" For writing answers, show them how to add more details or another thought.

- **If you have a student who loves computers,** let him type papers instead of writing them.

- **For testing, see about getting students special testing accommodations** such as extra time or breaking tests apart into smaller sections. This can help students pace themselves. Students who just cannot control how much they write, or who cannot stop themselves from rushing through, may be able to take the test orally. Or, they may be able to type on the computer, either to slow themselves down or help them speed up their writing and get more on the page, depending on how good their typing skills are.